ed

Pocket Peace

Peace
always

Pocket Peace

Effective Practices for
Enlightened Living

ALLAN LOKOS

Jeremy P. Tarcher / Penguin
a member of Penguin Group (USA) Inc.
New York

JEREMY P. TARCHER/PENGUIN
Published by the Penguin Group
Penguin Group (USA) Inc., 375 Hudson Street, New York,
New York 10014, USA • Penguin Group (Canada), 90 Eglinton Avenue East,
Suite 700, Toronto, Ontario M4P 2Y3, Canada (a division of Pearson Penguin Canada Inc.) •
Penguin Books Ltd, 80 Strand, London WC2R 0RL, England •
Penguin Ireland, 25 St Stephen's Green, Dublin 2, Ireland (a division of
Penguin Books Ltd) • Penguin Group (Australia), 250 Camberwell Road,
Camberwell, Victoria 3124, Australia (a division of Pearson Australia
Group Pty Ltd) • Penguin Books India Pvt Ltd, 11 Community Centre,
Panchsheel Park, New Delhi-110 017, India • Penguin Group (NZ),
67 Apollo Drive, Rosedale, North Shore 0632, New Zealand
(a division of Pearson New Zealand Ltd) • Penguin Books (South Africa)
(Pty) Ltd, 24 Sturdee Avenue, Rosebank, Johannesburg 2196, South Africa

Penguin Books Ltd, Registered Offices: 80 Strand, London WC2R 0RL, England

Most Tarcher/Penguin books are available at special quantity discounts for bulk purchase for
sales promotions, premiums, fund-raising, and educational needs. Special books or book excerpts
also can be created to fit specific needs. For details, write Penguin Group (USA) Inc.
Special Markets, 375 Hudson Street, New York, NY 10014.

Library of Congress Cataloging-in-Publication Data
Lokos, Allan.
Pocket peace : effective practices for enlightened living / Allan Lokos.
p.   cm.
ISBN 978-1-58542-781-9
1. Spiritual life—Meditations.   I. Title.
BL624.2.L65   2010   2009042704
204'.32—dc22

Printed in the United States of America
1 3 5 7 9 10 8 6 4 2

Book design by Jennifer Daddio

Neither the publisher nor the author is engaged in rendering professional advice or services
to the individual reader. The ideas, procedures, and suggestions contained in this book are not
intended as a substitute for consulting with your physician. All matters regarding your health require
medical supervision. Neither the author nor the publisher shall be liable or responsible for any
loss or damage allegedly arising from any information or suggestion in this book.

While the author has made every effort to provide accurate telephone numbers and Internet addresses
at the time of publication, neither the publisher nor the author assumes any responsibility for errors,
or for changes that occur after publication. Further, the publisher does not have any control over
and does not assume any responsibility for author or third-party websites or their content.

To Susanna,
with Love and Gratitude

Contents

Pocket Peace

Foreword

I f we stop and listen, become still and quiet enough to be rightly awed by the nature of our lives, we invariably find ourselves in conversation with some small voice, close and familiar, calling us to become better people, to be wiser, more focused, clear, at peace.

This deep listening, this call, this ache to be good and whole, is not as particularly noteworthy as it is ordinary. After all, this is what we are made for. To be cleansed of greed, anger, and hate. To be awake. To be happy and at peace. To give, receive, become love.

But if we are blessed, and somehow find ourselves

in this becalmed state of heart, we may find yet another challenge awaits us: What do we do now?

Here, we will undoubtedly feel an ancient pull in one of two seemingly opposite directions. Does our spiritual nature call us to retreat farther and farther from the noise and chaos of a world seemingly bent on its own destruction? And there pray, meditate, and calm our hearts, chanting ancient and sacred teachings, one less soldier in the war, quietly sending our healing, freely offering our own inner peace?

Or, newly awake in the power of love, does our love become action, our words become flesh, and our spiritual practice and our kindness suddenly inseparable, as we roll up our sleeves to do what we can to heal the sick, bind up the wounded, feed the hungry, comfort the bereaved?

Tending the inner life of our spirit and lovingly offering our generosity in the world are inseparable as the breath—the inhale and the exhale. Both are required for life to continue, to grow. Sadly, too many teachers and traditions tend to favor one over the other, insisting that either inner or outer practice is in some way morally or spiritually superior. This ridiculous, wastefully indulgent conflict has plagued and paralyzed seekers, teachers, traditions, and communities of people everywhere.

Thankfully for us, Allan Lokos is magnificently unin-terested in the timeless and seductive false choice between spiritual contemplation and spiritual action. Like all good teachers, he ignores both sides altogether and, taking our hand, guides us gently and confidently into the heart of the matter: a simple moment of attention, a day well spent, a life well lived.

Allan will say he is a student of Buddhism, which is surely true. He also loves music, cadence, simplicity, grace, wonder, and his luminous wife, Susanna. I have never seen him feel any need to choose among them. This is his gift to us: His intoxicating certainty that the smallest, simplest, next right thing is never a difficult choice. It is simply the next right thing.

In *Pocket Peace*, Allan walks us through the world, asks us to pay attention, to stay awake inside and out, and fills our pockets to overflowing with small, good things to do. Because it matters what we do. Ask the Buddha, ask Jesus, ask Mohammed, ask Mother Teresa, ask Black Elk. Through these and other teachers, Allan offers us this fiercely compassionate clarity: No matter who we are, what we believe, how sweet or beautiful our thoughts or ideas, when we step onto the land—into the street, the marketplace, the world—it matters what we do.

In the Christian New Testament, James writes a letter

directly challenging a growing sentiment in the young church (a sentiment still wildly popular today) that our spiritual faith is what heals us, rendering service to others—what we do in the world—of little consequence:

> *What does it profit, my brethren, if a man says he has faith but has not works? Can his faith save him? If a brother or sister is ill-clad and in lack of daily food, and one of you says to them, "Go in peace, be warmed and filled," without giving them the things needed for the body, what does it profit? So faith by itself, if it has no works, is dead.*

> James 2:14–17, RSV

For Allan Lokos, as for us, this is not merely a theological issue. Every time Allan walks out his door in New York City, the character in this biblical story shows up right in front of him as a real, living person. If we, too, are to be real, living people, we have no choice but to learn to breathe, inhale and exhale, to pay attention and be kind, stay awake and offer what we can, find peace in our hearts and offer it easily and joyfully to the first distressing face we encounter.

For anyone else, a life so well balanced, well lived, and in harmony would seem impossible—a high wire act.

Luckily for us, Allan has been crossing these busy streets his entire life. It feels good to follow him, and closely, for he seems to know the easiest, most playful way to the other side.

Wayne Muller
Santa Fe
August 2009

Introduction

Truths can be bitter and big; facts can be cold and hard. To be useful, facts need to be learned, so that you know, for instance, how many tables to ship when someone orders a gross, or how to create a table in Microsoft Excel, or how to set a table for an elegant dinner party. I find truths more interesting than facts. They usually address bigger questions, such as: What is the purpose of life? Who am I? Is there a God? Was it I who chopped down that cherry tree in a previous life? When truth and fact are in conflict, as they can be in important matters, I tend to side with truth because even relative truths are more stable than absolute facts, which seem to change on a daily basis with little or no warning. (Is broccoli still good for us? I can't remember.) In any event, truths and facts can be weighty stuff and especially difficult to untangle when life is coming at you quickly with both major and minor challenges, as it so regularly does. We often need to be quick on our feet—or perhaps, more accurately, quick of mind—able to respond in an instant to a challenging situation or earth-shattering news. To do that, we need a clear sense of who we are and what matters most to us. We must be well acquainted with our ethical center, or what I call our *true self*.

We live in a turbulent world struggling to find peace. There is a spiritual yearning so deep and pervasive that at times it is palpable, at other times subtle, barely simmering, yet its anxiety and unrest are ever-present. Even when all the pieces seem to be in place—good health, loving relationships, a rewarding career—it can still feel like something is wrong, unsettled, missing. We struggle to find meaning in a life that at times feels empty, fearful, and uncertain. We know we don't want to get sucked into the shadows of anger, fear, and greed, but they surround us and beckon to us. Within this setting, each of us is looking for what all sentient beings want, and have always wanted. To put it most simply, we want to be happy. We yearn for there to be meaning to our lives, balanced with a sense of inner peace and joy.

I am one of those fortunate people who enjoy remarkably good health. I rarely get a cold, and when I do, typically it lasts no more than a day or two. Not long ago my wife, Susanna, and I saw a wonderful performance of *Iphigénie en Tauride* at the Metropolitan Opera in New York. As we were leaving the opera house I felt a kind of tingling sensation high up in my chest, near the esophagus. I'm not familiar with the feeling of indigestion, but it seemed to me that this was what it would feel like. It lasted about twenty minutes and, although uncomfortable, there was no pain, and once it stopped there seemed to be no cause for concern. Later, at about five a.m., I went to the bathroom, and suddenly there was great cause for concern. Standing there, I felt light-headed and slightly nauseated. I grabbed the towel bar in front of me for support, but the next thing I knew I was flat out on the floor with the towel bar ripped out of the wall, clutched in my hands. Susanna, awakened by my crash to the floor, was at my side in an instant. We were now both in uncharted waters. My cold, sweaty head and extremely pale complexion raised concerns in Susanna about the possibility of a heart attack, so despite my protestations, she wisely dialed 911 and asked for help. Within minutes two policemen and two EMS crews were at my side. (It must have been a slow night in the world of New York City emergencies.)

The ambulance ride, accompanied by the shrieking whine of a siren and the squeal of tires as we turned corners, went quickly through the cold, dark night. I had at that point returned to a state of clearheadedness and was being entertained by one of the EMS fellows' views as to why the Patriots would finish the season unbeaten. In the emergency room I was soon surrounded by a number of what seemed to me teenage *Grey's Anatomy* wannabes. I was hearing the term "atrial fibrillation" being murmured between them as their dewy glances alternated between me and the monitor to which I was now wired. ("Atrial fibrillation" is an abnormal heart rhythm involving the two upper chambers of the heart. The heart goes out of sync with its natural pacemaker, and because blood is not being pumped properly, clots can form and there is a considerable risk of stroke.) The monitor was showing wildly erratic numbers up into the 180s, and the graphic readout of my heartbeat was bouncing around like a vervet monkey on vodka. An older doctor (must have been at least thirty) arrived and told me that one standard method of dealing with such conditions is to sedate the patient, run a wire up from the groin, and shock the heart so that it re-syncs back to normal function. It didn't sound awful, especially since I would be asleep, but it wouldn't have been my first choice to add to a day that otherwise had been going along in such jolly fashion.

It was now about ten a.m., and we were told that it would be anywhere from four to ten hours before a room would be available for me, so I decided to put the time to good use. I had, at that point, more than a decade of formal meditation practice and had been blessed with the opportunity to work with a number of the world's great teachers. In fact, I was supposed to be with my current mentor, the renowned meditation teacher and author Sharon Salzberg, at that very time, so a formal sitting right then and there seemed perfect. (What could be a better place for meditation than a hospital emergency room?) As I began, Susanna pointed out that using my heart as an object of concentration might be beneficial, and I agreed. (An object of concentration is simply something on which one focuses the mind. Typically, it might be the breath, but it can be most anything.)

About forty minutes later I sensed that we were no longer alone in our little cubicle. I opened my eyes to find the young interns quizzically looking at me, then checking my monitor and my chart—back and forth, me, monitor, chart, me, monitor, chart. Then one of them asked, "You *are* Mr. Lokos, aren't you?" I replied, "Yes," because in spite of the confusion of the day, I still felt that I was who I thought I was. The interns left and returned a short while later with a resident cardiologist who went through the same routine—monitor, chart, me, monitor, chart, me. All of the fuss was about the fact that apparently, while in meditation, I had unknowingly caused my heart to return to normal function, something not unheard of but also not that common. Evidently, these young folks had not seen this before. All I did was what I do each morning at the beginning of my meditation practice—brought my mind and body to a quiet, stable state of calm. Meditators refer to this state as *samatha,* a Sanskrit word meaning "calm abiding."

I was kept in the hospital overnight even though there was no treatment necessary or appropriate for me. (One well-intentioned nurse woke me at about four a.m. and presented me with some pills that were actually supposed to go to the fellow in the next bed.) The next day I was released from the hospital with a recommendation that I see a cardiologist within the next week or two. Following orders, a few days later I had a thorough examination by Dr. Hartcheck, which included a stress test and attachment to various impressive-looking machines known only by letters, a kind of medical alphabet soup. The good doctor put me on medication for the fibrillation (although it had stopped) and a blood thinner to protect against the possibility of a stroke (which was unlikely without the fibrillation). A few weeks later I was attached to a small halter monitor, which I was to wear at home for twenty-four hours. Using the information obtained from the monitor, Dr. H. determined, to my delight, that I was recovered and could come off all medication.

The use of meditation (not medication) in this instance is an example of what, for me, was a practice I could pull from my pocket at any time. However, it was quickly accessible only because of my years of study and practice of meditation. The practices that you will be reading about in the ensuing pages do not require long periods of study or strenuous effort. However, like most worthwhile endeavors, you will find that what you put into these practices will be reflected in what you get out of them. That being said, folks have reported to me that even a few minutes working with just one of these practices has brought insight, increased happiness, decreased stress, and given them a brighter outlook on life. Indeed, I have heard the word "transformative" used to describe them more than once.

This is not a meditation manual (there are several excellent ones available), and all of the practices herein can be used to great benefit by non-meditators. However, in a sense, each of the practices offered here is a form of meditation, in that they require one to be aware of one's thoughts, words, and actions as they are occurring in the moment.

You and I are simply a process—a phenomenon of vibrating energy dependent on, and responding to, an ongoing, continually unfolding series of contingent events and conditions. No matter how much we may like or dislike these conditions, they will all change. In fact, they are constantly changing and ultimately will fade away, as you and I are changing in every subparticle of every moment and will also fade away, at least from this life form. Don't be concerned if you've never thought about things this way. You have been living with this constant change—the law of impermanence—all your life. It is this very arising and passing of phenomena that can inspire our greatest thoughts and deeds and arouse the desire to explore life's deepest truths. The rapidity of life's unfolding events often calls for us to be able to respond quickly, yet without the conditioned responses and habitual knee-jerk reactions that can cause sorrow for ourselves and others. We want to be in the world in such a way that even in the heat of a moment, the person we want to be is fully present, compassionate, and wise. Through that level of awareness our highest ideals flourish and our ethical self, our true self, evolves.

The teachings of our great spiritual leaders, scholars, and philosophers are invaluable in guiding us on our journey. Yet they are only guides—we need more. No, wait, let's rethink that. Perhaps what we need is less. When we need to think, speak, or act quickly, we want to be carrying less, not more. When life is coming at us like a freight train, we need short, concise practices that can help us think, speak, and act wisely under pressure. I call these *Pocket Practices*—small but effective practices that we develop slowly so that we can call on them quickly, instinctively. They are light, responsive, and powerful. There is no magic offered here, nor are there secret formulas, just common sense and great spiritual teachings distilled into concentrated dosages—wisdom of the ages practiced, ready, and honed for use in the modern world. These practices are based on the Buddhist teachings called "*Paramis*," or Perfection Practices. Each of the Paramis—or, in this instance, their Pocket Practice versions—supports the others. Generosity supports relinquishing, which supports moral behavior, which supports truthfulness, which supports patience, which supports wisdom, which supports equanimity, and so forth. It is a cycle of practices that can lead to happiness and enlightened living for people of all beliefs, or no particular beliefs at all. This is not "spirituality lite" but rather "spirituality pragmatic."

The key to the value of the Pocket Practices is understanding them as *practices*. They are not something to believe in, as a religion or a spiritual tradition, nor are they a panacea, a cure-all to eliminate personal issues or the ills of the world. A practice is something we do. It's not about codes, philosophies, or dogmas. A practice can never be assumed to be learned. We may get better at it, but we must always practice the practice if it is to be useful, just as we must walk the talk if it is to be meaningful. Soon you may find yourself joyfully ready to practice at every appropriate opportunity.

An advanced spiritual practitioner can still become sad, angry, ill, and disappointed. We cannot change much of what comes at us in life, and we don't want to suppress feelings and emotions, but we can change our responses to, and experience of, life's situations. The importance of this type of practice, which is in truth a form of mind training, is understood as we become aware that the very quality of our lives is determined by how we experience the events, situations, and conditions within and around us. Some of these practices will help you respond with greater wisdom to life's challenging moments, while others will help you enjoy greater peace, fulfillment, and a more joyful life.

I spent the first thirty years of my adult life in the arts as a professional singer on Broadway and in concert and opera. I also taught singers, produced and directed a number of theatrical productions, and even started a successful artist-management company. Then, for reasons probably best described as a "calling," this gallivanting agnostic entered a seminary and emerged a few years later as an ordained Interfaith minister. (Susanna vowed that she would never follow such a path, but, to the amusement and delight of us both, was ordained two years later.) In the aftermath of the events of September 11, 2001, we cofounded the organization that would become the Community Meditation Center in New York City. Inspired by our own life-changing experiences with Buddhist meditation and the growing interest in meditation in the Western world, we looked to create a nondogmatic, welcoming atmosphere for personal spiritual exploration supported by a creative, open-minded community. I am grateful to the members of the Community for their willingness to enthusiastically try these Pocket Practices and share their experiences with me. They have helped polish these little gems to their current form.

From the perspective of thirty years in the creative arts and another ten in active ministry and meditation practice, I've come to believe that true creativity is a spiritual experience, and likewise, spirituality can inspire our greatest creativity. I don't think that can be said of our world religions. Religious institutions are dedicated to preserving the sanctity of the original teachings of their faith. Therefore, creativity, originality, and imaginative thinking can be in opposition to religious establishment. Whatever creative thinking comes out of religious circles more often than not manifests as a new denomination of an existing form. However, for those looking to be in touch with their spiritual essence, those looking for a sense of equanimity in their lives and the experience of inner peace, the creative spirit can enhance and inspire the adventure. It can provide the juice for the journey. The very nature of these Pocket Practices encourages creativity and an imaginative approach.

I find myself less and less enamored with philosophies and theories about how to live a meaningful life, and more and more interested in practices that address the realities of everyday life. In real life there is heavy traffic when we're late, the office can be hell, relationships go through stress, viruses and cancers take up residence in our bodies, and loved ones get sick and die, as will we.

There's a line I like about the difference between religion and spirituality: "Religion is for those who are afraid of going to hell; spirituality is for those who have already been there." We've all experienced turmoil and sorrow, and we've all lived with the consequences of anger, greed, and delusion—our own and that of others. We know what it's like to feel frightened, humiliated, envious, and depressed. We know what hell feels like.

I live in New York City. There are those who say that the pursuit of kindness, compassion, joy, and inner peace in this bustling, materialistic *mecca-to-the-mega* town is especially challenging. Perhaps, but for me it has opened up opportunities to create small yet powerful practices that can be used in the impatient, confusing, and occasional harshness of real life—practices I've found to be just as valuable in quieter, more sedate surroundings as well. Some uplift the spirit and provide a method for dealing with disappointments, anger, insecurity, reactive patterns, and judgmental tendencies. Others awaken and support our kinder, more compassionate, more generous self. I devote considerable time each day to my formal meditation practice, but I also keep my Pocket Practices honed and ready for immediate use as needed. They don't require a meditation cushion, sacred space, candles, incense, or a holy attitude, just a desire for a greater sense of peace, happiness, and enlightenment. Some of the practices are recommended for use on a daily basis, while others can be effective when worked just once or twice a year. After trying the recommended schedule, feel free to create your own.

I have created these practices based on the teachings of those who have preceded me, dating back more than two thousand five hundred years, and as I share them with you I encourage you to use your imagination and mold them so that they can best serve you on your journey. As the Buddha said, "You should decide . . . not by what you have heard, not by following convention, not by assuming it is so, not by relying on the texts, not because of reasoning, not because of logic, not by thinking about explanations, not by acquiescing to the views that you prefer, not because it appears likely, and not just out of respect for a teacher. When you would know . . . for yourselves, that these things are unhealthy . . . then . . . you should reject them. These things are healthy . . . you should stay with them" (Anguttara 3:65).

Needless to say, the road will not always be smooth. In 1969, the Chicago Cubs, a Major League baseball team that has endured considerable suffering through most of the twentieth and twenty-first centuries, appeared to be on their way to winning the National League pennant. They had a big lead in the standings and, as they approached the end of the season, victory was in sight. Then they lost a few games, and those losses led to a complete collapse. The New York Mets overcame them and won the pennant. Afterward, Leo Durocher, the Cubs' fiery and astute manager, said that the Cubs lost the pennant because they didn't know how to lose games. This seemingly odd statement revealed a deep wisdom. While his team was winning, everything was fine, but when faced with a few setbacks, they began to doubt themselves and lost their way. In spiritual practice we face the same challenge. Every experienced practitioner knows that they will make mistakes and speak or act unskillfully, sometimes right after a beautiful meditation session. That's why it is called "practice." Instead of losing faith, we get back up, accept our humanity, learn from our slipups, and return to our winning ways. Unlike in baseball, our game is never lost.

It may seem surprising, but spiritual practice is not about becoming a better person. You are already whole and perfect as you are. Spiritual practice is about becoming present to that perfection. Mindfulness is the quality that opens the door to the presence of our true self. We become present to what is happening within us and around us as it is happening. Therefore these practices are intended to help us become more aware of our thoughts, feelings, perceptions, and motivations, and to see things as they really are, not as they appear to be.

May you reap joy and peace from your efforts, and may you share your true self with all beings.

Generosity

sparrow gives its song
only awakened ears hear
distance means nothing
—MICHO

I n spite of my many years of productive work in psy-
chotherapy, I don't remember a great deal about my
childhood, but there is an incident that has remained
with me for more than half a century. Our family occasionally had lunch on Sundays at a popular neighborhood restaurant. (The concept of "brunch" had not been
conceived as yet, or perhaps had not reached the far
shores of Brooklyn, New York, so "lunch" it was.) On one
particular Sunday, as we left the restaurant, there were
two women sitting at a table just outside the entrance.
They were dressed in costumes that this ten-year-old,

having been raised in, and limited to, a predominantly Jewish neighborhood, had never seen before. They were Catholic nuns. On the table was a glass bowl with a small amount of money in it, and as I walked past, one of them said gently, "Please help the poor." My allowance at that time was twenty-five cents a week, and I had six weeks' worth in my pocket. I took my six quarters and placed them in the bowl. The ladies smiled, thanked me, and said, "God bless you." As I walked away I felt warm and special inside, and very grown-up, feelings to which I was not accustomed. My father, having caught the tail end of the exchange, realized what I had done and quickly yanked me by the arm. His fury, to which I *was* well accustomed, flared up, and in a growly whisper he demanded, "Did you give them money?" I nodded that I had. He barked his angry reply, "We don't do that!" as he yanked me harder by the arm. I wanted to ask what I had done wrong, but I was too frightened, a feeling to which I was also well accustomed, so I never learned what it was we didn't do. Was I not supposed to give money away, or not give to a religion different from ours, or not give to women in penguin-like costumes, or . . . Actually, I never could come up with another possibility. I do know that I was left with a lesson firmly communicated—I had committed a serious error, and it was not to be repeated.

Years later I learned that my father had a great many significant things taken from him in his youth. He was removed from school at an early age to help run the family business, so he never was able to fulfill his dream of becoming a doctor. The business grew and became quite successful, but then all was lost in the Great Depression and he was left with nothing. As an adult he was able to support his family, but any innate qualities of generosity never developed. Also, unbeknownst to me, the underpinnings of a serious mental illness were there, and it would become more debilitating throughout his life.

What I also didn't know at the time was that although the message of my misdeed had been made abundantly clear, my intuitive act of generosity was noble, kind, and an honorable endeavor. The feeling of openhearted joy that I had experienced in that moment was powerful and, although squelched, ultimately would not be denied. It was many years later that I learned that generosity is one of the main practices from which all spiritual growth emanates, and it is the energy with which spiritual development flourishes. Generosity is compelling, and we increase its power when we offer a kind word, a compassionate ear, or material gifts such as food, clothing, or money.

More than two thousand five hundred years ago, no less a sage than the Buddha taught how important it is to develop an open heart and a generous spirit. In naming the virtuous practices that lead the way to enlightenment, a listing that includes morality, wisdom, truthfulness, and lovingkindness, he placed generosity at the very top of the list. From this we might conclude that one cannot begin to lead a moral life with a heart that is closed to the needs of others. In the Judeo-Christian tradition, generosity is considered mandatory. There is a story about a yeshiva student who asked a rabbi if, on a given day, he didn't feel generous in his heart, did he have to act against his feelings and give anyway? The rabbi said, "The hungry must be fed today, not just when we're in the mood." Then he added, "Acts of generosity open a constricted heart."

The Buddha saw that all beings want to be happy and that even the simplest act of generosity could free us from the fear of not having enough; it also loosens the shackles of endless greed and obsessiveness. "If beings knew, as I know, the results of giving and sharing," said the Buddha, "they would not eat without having given. . . . Even if it were their last bite, they would not eat without having shared" (Itivuttaka 18).

Unfortunately, most of us are bombarded with such an array of appeals from worthy causes that the joy of giving can metamorphose into what feels like an assault on our spirit, our wallets, and our energy. The phone rings with recorded appeals, and earnest requests by e-mail are more and more pervasive. The mailbox is jammed with pleas from important causes at holiday time (which used to begin a month before Christmas and now seems to begin a month after Christmas—for the next holiday season). City dwellers are approached by unfortunate beings with their hands out on every street corner. Television and newspaper accounts of individuals, groups, and countries in desperate need can leave us distraught, saddened, and numb. It is understandable that our hearts might harden without our realizing that we have cut ourselves off from our fellow beings who are most in need of our generosity. Through this lens my father's fear, while not particularly enlightened, can be viewed with compassion.

I once read about a teacher in a privileged private school who asked her fifth-grade class to write an essay about poverty. One ten-year-old began his by writing, "Once there was a very poor family. They were so poor that the butler was poor, the maids were poor, and both chauffeurs were poor." For the vast majority of us, wealth or poverty is very much a matter of perspective. I once heard the Vietnamese Zen Buddhist monk Thich Nhat Hanh say that when an American says he is hungry, it's usually because he arrived home late for dinner.

What are the obstacles that come between us and the instinct to help? While there are a number of answers, I think they all begin with fear. We may fear that we won't have enough for ourselves, or that the cause before us is not really worthy or honest. We may resent (a form of fear) those who are needy and making our neighborhood (and therefore us) look less appealing. We may fear the people asking for our help because they don't look like us or because their customs (or costumes) are different from ours. It is easy to find reasons not to be generous. Unfortunately, none of them bring happiness to ourselves or anyone else. So, how can we rekindle the joy of a generous heart in a practical and meaningful way?

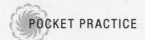 POCKET PRACTICE

For one week carry at least five one-dollar bills with you wherever you go, and do not walk past anyone who is asking for help.

During this week, make eye contact with every home-less person, or those in any way down on their luck who reach out for your help. Engage in a short conversation: "How are you doing?" is a good starter. Give them a dol-lar and wish them well. The specific amount can vary in accordance with your resources, but not by judging the recipient's worthiness. This exercise needs to be done in a completely nonjudgmental way. It's easy to rationalize that the downtrodden might use your generosity for drink or drugs, or that anyone who really wants to can find a job, but for this practice leave out the suppositions. After all, we don't know. We can never really know someone else's story. It would be better to be fooled by a hundred con men than to bypass one worthy being. Try it for a week. Just practice generosity. Be more generous than you have ever been. Give for the sake of giving; be totally indiscriminate; get intoxicated with the joy of generosity. Once a year for a week, engage in this type of wholesale generosity and note what it feels like.

To be completely honest, the practice can be addictive. People have reported to me that once they had done it for a week they found themselves unwilling to give up the joy of face-to-face sharing. One woman told me that this practice helped her get over her fear of a local homeless man, and now she looks forward to her chat with Tommy each morning. Another shared with me that giving so freely led her to realize how much she had. While she is not particularly wealthy, she learned that she always had enough to share with others, which made her feel rich. My own experience has been that so many times when I give a homeless person a dollar and a moment of myself, they often respond by saying, "God bless you." We all like bargains. A heartfelt blessing for a dollar—that is a good deal. Yes, you may occasionally run into a person who responds to your gift by expressing dissatisfaction with the amount you gave, or does not respond at all. That's okay, your part is to practice generosity. How your gift is received is up to the recipient. When an act of generosity is genuinely altruistic, it is free of expectations and therefore the response of the recipient is seen as unimportant. One more point: if you find you are too busy to spend a moment with people who are down on their luck, perhaps you're too busy.

There is an old Hasidic tale about a man who lived in a small village and was known for his generosity. It was said that no one who came to his door left empty-handed. One day a beggar appeared, and the kindly man was dismayed because he had absolutely nothing in the house. Then he remembered a gold watch he had put away in a drawer years ago. He got it out and gave it to the beggar. When his wife saw what he had done she yelled at him, "Are you crazy? That watch is worth hundreds. Call that beggar back." So the man called out, "Hey, you, come back here." The beggar came back, and the man said to him, "That watch is worth hundreds. When you sell it, be sure to get a good price." That man was not only generous, he was wise and had an understanding of the real worth of things.

Of course, all cities and towns have their unique attributes, and you may live where you don't often encounter street people, homeless folks, or beggars. To work with this Pocket Practice, simply use your imagination and expand the parameters. Go to places that could benefit from your generosity and make a contribution regularly. See if you can spend a few minutes with one or two of the needy folk. If that isn't possible, adopt a generous attitude toward the appeals that come in the mail or online. On certain websites you can contribute with the click of a mouse. Some of them don't even require that you give money—just a click and advertisers will contribute. Perhaps for a year, make a five-dollar contribution each month to one of the causes that you may have previously ignored. Again, bypass judgment and simply give. A five-dollar donation once a month adds up to sixty dollars for the entire year. Whatever the amount, the object is to practice giving; it is a practice whose value is priceless.

Not long ago, my brother Harry died after a protracted illness that attacked his body for twenty-eight years. His condition first appeared one morning while he was enjoying his daily jog. It began as numbness in his left leg, causing it to become unresponsive and heavy, and as time went by he was walking with a noticeable limp. After a few years he reluctantly began using a cane. Then two canes became necessary in order for him to get around. All through this time he continued to work actively and play golf and even tennis—moving from singles to doubles as his mobility decreased. On the golf course, he would steady himself with two crutches under his arms and drive the ball with consistent accuracy, and although his game became shorter, he loved playing and his enthusiasm was a joyful reminder to his friends that there can be more to a game than just the score. Propped up on two crutches, Harry actually hit a hole in one and was voted *man of the year* in his Floridian community. Surely not even Tiger Woods could have been more ecstatic. Eventually, Harry had no choice but to yield to a wheelchair, which became his mode of transportation for the last ten years of his life. In those latter years his condition gradually overtook his entire body, and by the last year, even eating was a major challenge.

Harry wasn't a movie star, a politician, or any other type of celebrity, nor was he a particularly religious or spiritual person, but when he died some four hundred people attended his funeral. Over and over again, people said the same thing to me about my brother: "Harry always greeted me with a smile and asked how I was doing." This, of course, from his wheelchair. A number of people told me how Harry inspired them with his ubiquitous smile. They knew he had serious physical challenges with which he had to contend every moment of every day. The basics that most of us take for granted—getting a glass of water, going to the bathroom, shaving, traveling, turning around—all presented issues. But no one ever heard him complain—they knew only his smile and friendly greeting. And when people told me about their particular experience of Harry and his smile, they smiled, many with tears in their eyes, and I had the sense that he would be remembered for a very long time.

 POCKET PRACTICE

Greet folks with a smile.

No matter what your mood or the circumstances of the moment, it is almost always possible to conjure up a smile. This is not meant to be a form of denial but rather a way to make the world a more joyful place, and a reminder to ourselves that there is more to life than our current difficulties. You can brighten the day for others, and that has to be good for you as well. Imagine, every time you cross paths with someone you can both get a little lift from your smile. I have been consciously doing this practice for a number of years, and during that time—life being what it is—I have had my share of serious issues with which to deal, the death of my only brother being but one of them. Yet every smile as I greet someone, or simply cross someone's path, has lightened whatever distress or care has been within me. The smile that is usually returned has often lifted me right out of my concerns. Issues don't evaporate as if by magic, but our perspective can change and life will become brighter. No economic crisis can devalue a smile, and it might be just the stimulus package a friend needs.

A few years ago, my wife, Susanna, suddenly began running a high fever, which at night would spike to more than 104 degrees. Our doctor was baffled, and after a couple of days we found ourselves checking in at the hospital. After a few more days an entire medical team was baffled. Tests were being run, guesses were being offered by everyone, but no answers. The doctors expressed amazement at some of the astonishing numbers that were coming back from her tests, but still no answers. My daily routine during this time became: rise early, walk the dog, and head for the hospital. After a few hours, I would then go back across town for another dog walk and general check-in at home, and then back to the hospital. On one of those runs, when I gave the taxi driver the hospital address, he asked if I was a doctor. When I explained about my wife he was quiet for a while, and then he reached up to the rearview mirror, where a long set of prayer beads hung. He handed them to me and asked that I give them to my wife. He assured me that they would help. He had been praying with them for many years, and Allah had always been good to him. He also refused to accept payment for the ride, saying it was his way of giving thanks in advance for my wife's recovery. That night, Susanna's fever went down and stayed down. Two days later she was discharged from the hospital with no diagnosis, no medication, and, most important, no symptoms. I have no way of knowing what, if anything, that taxi driver's generosity contributed to Susanna's recovery. I do know that he gave us a tremendous lift during a difficult time, a lift we have never forgotten.

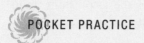

POCKET PRACTICE

Perform spontaneous acts of generosity.

It might feel a bit awkward at first, but most of us find it exhilarating to let go of inhibition. It can take a bit of practice, but the desire to be both spontaneous and generous already exists within you. Give yourself and those around you the joy of your generous heart.

I think the greatest gift any of us can offer to another is our complete presence. It is astonishing how many people go through life without anyone who truly listens to them. To become one who listens deeply, without judgment, without offering advice, without the need to be anything but fully, consciously present, is to become a great gift to all who cross your path. You might be the first person to actually listen to the human being who is speaking to you. You can, in such moments, change a life. When a life changes, the world changes.

POCKET PRACTICE

Focus intently on what is being said by others, so as to be able to repeat accurately what they have said.

Do this exercise with family members, friends, or anyone. Listen as closely as you can. Notice if you have a desire to respond with advice or an opinion. Gently let go of all that and just listen. It is unlikely that you could do this exercise all the time, so choose one or two conversations each day for a week and give it a try. This practice can actually be fun as well as deeply rewarding. It is a great honor to be known as one who truly listens.

POCKET PRACTICE

From time to time, when you want to ask for more, ask instead, "How can I give more?"

Also, sometimes, when you are about to say, "Things aren't being done the way I want," say instead, "How can I help?" Notice what it feels like to bypass your desires and open yourself up to the needs of others. Conversely, what does it feel like to be concerned primarily with your own needs and desires? Understand the difference, and encourage your generous self to flourish.

Whatever you give, give with a smile, gratitude for all you have, and respect for the recipient. Whenever we are asked to give, it is an opportunity to practice generosity, which leads naturally to freedom, joy, and enlightenment. The person who asks for your help is, therefore, offering you a great gift. We come to see that the giver and the receiver are one.

Morality

wind gusts decide the
snow that will drift I only
steer best as able
—MICHO

One of the perks you receive if you become a subscriber to the Metropolitan Opera in New York City is that you can exchange any performance on your subscription for any other performance that season. To make the privilege even juicier, exchanges and additional purchases can be made one week before tickets go on sale to the general public. After several years of not subscribing, Susanna and I realized that we missed the magnificent music and the grand nights out and decided to subscribe for the new season. On the first day that ticket exchanges could be made, I headed down to the opera house. Within a few minutes I was in a conversation with the woman on line in front of me, who, it turned out, was not a subscriber. She and her husband and another couple always went to the Met on New Year's Eve. Her dilemma was that she needed to buy four tickets but was leaving town later that day for a month and knew there would be no tickets left for that special night when she returned. She was hoping that the ticket seller would make an exception and let her buy tickets that morning, even though she was not a subscriber. We both agreed it was a long shot, but then I suddenly realized I could help her. I told her that if they wouldn't sell her the tickets, I would buy them for her and she could simply buy them from me. She was thrilled; what could have been better? I would have the pleasure of helping a fellow being, and she and her friends would enjoy their traditional New Year's Eve at the opera.

When she got to the ticket seller, he told her that only subscribers could buy tickets that day and he couldn't make an exception. She backed away, and I stepped up and asked for four tickets for New Year's Eve. He offered me a couple of choices and I turned to the woman and asked which she wanted. The ticket seller then stopped me and pointed out that if I bought the tickets for the woman I would be abusing a privilege reserved for subscribers, and that a subscriber who might have wanted those tickets would not be able to get them. I felt taken aback and perplexed. I thought I was doing a good deed, but it turned out that if I did, I would be breaking the rules— and it seemed to me that the rules were perfectly fair. Besides, no matter what I thought, if you play a game you should play by the rules. With good intentions, I had spoken before thinking, and my potential good deed could end up depriving someone of what would otherwise have been legitimately theirs. I looked at the woman, who was hoping I'd keep my word to her, and the ticket seller, who was hoping I'd do the right thing for the legitimate subscribers, and realized that I had a decision to make, and that morality was not always a straightforward matter. Someone else might have had no question in their mind as to what the right decision should have been, but I had considerable conflict.

I presented this story in a talk I offered at the Community Meditation Center. I then asked everyone to take a moment to consider what they would have done had they been in my position. Next, I asked for a show of hands—a vote to determine if there was a clear leaning in one direction or the other. It turned out that the vote was almost dead even. Then came the interesting part. I asked everyone to change their mind and see the argument from the other side. I saw smiles begin to appear on faces as folks realized that truly considering the other side is something we don't tend to do very often. (Our teenage children will gladly point this out to us.)

Stop reading for a moment and weigh both sides and decide what you would have done. When you have decided and believe you are right, try changing your mind (for real) and convince yourself that the other side of the argument is right. This is only an exercise, so remember to have fun with it.

Morality, as a fixed set of principles concerning the distinction between right and wrong or good and bad, is necessary for a stabilized society, but as a solidified code, or a doctrine of absolutes, it does not, in my view, encourage awareness or thoughtful, ethical exploration. I believe it can be beneficial to appreciate the feelings of inner peace and satisfaction that come from making a wise, considered decision in a difficult situation—a choice not necessarily viewed as "right" by others but that is in keeping with the actions of an awakened moral being. I like to think of that type of action, and the ensuing feelings, as expressions of our highest self. Most of us are pretty good at beating ourselves up—an unwise and unproductive use of energy—when we make a poor choice. Why not allow the pleasant, peaceful feelings associated with wise moral decisions to massage the spirit?

Being able to make choices in the heat of the moment that are in accord with our ethical self becomes easier when we regularly spend quiet time with ourselves considering what is important to us. Developing our own moral self requires more of us than accepting the values of others. We need to examine our own morality through the lens of our everyday activities, our society, backgrounds, aspirations, conditions, and responsibilities. It is our actions that count more than our beliefs. Most of us are unlikely to murder someone no matter how incensed we may become, but are we aware of the times we may have severely wounded the spirit of another with an angry word or a thoughtless deed? We are not likely to rob a bank at gunpoint, but do we consider it perfectly acceptable to bring home office supplies for our personal use, or to suddenly develop a poor memory at income-tax time? Do we cause harm by misusing our sexual energy? Do we ever speak in a way that is misleading, unkind, or divisive? Do we overindulge in intoxicants or medications that numb or alter the mind-state in order to ease the painful and unpleasant events of our day? It can be beneficial to view these questions in the light offered by the five basic precepts taught by the Buddha. They are intended to help us relieve anguish for ourselves and those around us and to promote peace of mind and peace in the community. They also shed light in those little dark places where we might not otherwise look. These precepts are: to refrain from killing or harming any living being; to refrain from taking anything that is not freely given; to refrain from sexual misconduct; to refrain from false, harmful, or harsh speech; and to refrain from abusing intoxicants that can cloud the mind.

A client told me about how she enjoyed her cup of Starbucks espresso roast each morning. Then, a few weeks after we had discussed the five precepts, she told me that she had regularly taken a handful of sweetener packets from the store once or twice a week to use at home. She hadn't thought anything about it before, but upon reflection it felt to her as though she were stealing. She now bought her sweetener from the market and found that every time she did, it brought a smile to her face. She said she didn't realize that she felt sneaky before, and now she was free of that darkness. There is freedom and joy in ethical behavior.

There is a story in the Buddhist teachings that shows how breaking one precept, even a bit, can lead to a moral breakdown. A monk was traveling, and as was the custom, he would offer teachings in exchange for food and lodging. On one occasion he was offered lodging by a young woman who lived alone. She made her offer conditional on his having to do one of three things: sleep with her, sacrifice a goat, or drink alcohol. The weather was harsh and he had no other shelter, so he accepted her offer and decided on the alcohol, thinking that a drink would be the least harmful of the choices. However, one drink led to another, and before long he was drunk. At that point, the bleating sound of the goat annoyed him so much that he killed it, and when he woke up in the morning he found himself in bed with the woman.

Feeling guilty about mistakes we have made does nothing to move us in a positive direction. If it is possible to apologize for an unskillful action or poor choice of words, we should do so. It can heal relationships, lighten the heart, and help us be more mindful of our thoughts, words, and deeds in the future. But remember that there is no guarantee that our apology will be graciously received. All we can do is be sincere, learn from our unskillfulness, and be more present while going forward.

bought the tickets for the woman that day. I was probably influenced by the fact that she was standing right in front of me and I would have been upset by her disappointment had I not bought them for her. The people who possibly (okay, probably) would have wanted the tickets were not there and I didn't have to face their disappointment, but at least I made one person and her friends happy. Perhaps someday I may have the opportunity to do something kind for the people (having no idea who they are) who never got to buy those tickets. Morally correct decisions are not always clear, but I felt clean about the choice I made, even realizing that an hour later I might have made a different one. According to Buddhist thought, the karmic result of an action comes about from the intention that motivates the action. The teachings use words like "wholesome" and "unwholesome" rather than "right" and "wrong." My intention was to help someone. I saw how I should have paused to think before jumping in with my offer, but once in the predicament, I made my decision based on what felt like wholesome intention.

Examining morality and benefiting from practices that support our beliefs require a clear understanding of our intention and motivation in specific circumstances. Several years ago, I worked for a not-for-profit organization. I enjoyed my job, my colleagues, and the sense that my time and efforts were being used productively. I admired Zack, the person for whom I worked directly, and over time we had become friends. He, it turned out, was becoming increasingly dissatisfied with the organization's directors, and when there suddenly came an opportunity for him to leave and consider other options, Zack was ready to act on it. He was joined by his old friend Beverly, who had the legal background to advise him and guide him through the process. If Zack wanted to move on, I, for one, was ready to follow him.

One day Zack brought Beverly to a staff meeting that, we were told, was an opportunity for each of us to share our feelings about the current situation—specifically, our thoughts about what we would do if Zack left the company. As people spoke, it appeared that if Zack did resign a number of the staff would likely leave as well. That caused me concern for the stability of the company. When my turn came to speak, I expressed my feeling that we should make all efforts to reconcile differences with the directors, since so many people resigning at the same time could cause turmoil for the organization and seriously disrupt business. Beverly interrupted me, stating that it would be highly unlikely that progress could ever be made with the current directors. I felt resentment arise in me for a moment as I thought, *If we're all here to share our feelings, why am I being corrected?* However, I said nothing and instead nodded in agreement.

Later, as Zack's displeasure became more out in the open, a meeting was scheduled for the staff and directors to sit down together and talk. Just before the meeting began, I learned that Zack was going to request that two key directors resign, and apparently, if they did not, he would resign. It seemed likely at that point that if he resigned, so would a substantial number of the rest of us. I felt uncomfortable with that strategy, knowing that these directors who had served the organization for many years were unlikely to agree to resign and the action that I did not favor was heading toward inevitability. My sense was that we were moving too quickly and were going to cause disruption and ill will that could possibly be avoided. Although Beverly had prepared some sort of proposal, I felt that we had never really negotiated in good faith to see if a peaceful resolution might be possible.

Friends of mine who do couples counseling have told me that often when couples come to them to work on their relationship, one party is there working for reconciliation, and the other, often without even realizing it, is there looking for divorce counseling. I think that was our situation—one party wanting out, the other looking to hold the organization together.

Of course, that is my memory of those difficult days, and I certainly recognize that others involved at the time might recall things differently. (Sometimes, when I would hear my brother's reminiscences of our childhood days,

I would wonder if we were raised in the same home.) Most of us are quite convinced that our recollection of things is completely accurate, even if the events took place twenty, thirty, or even fifty years ago. We argue, offering meticulous details of who said what, or who started what, as if that would settle the disagreement. It rarely does.

As I look back, I realize that no one could ever have known of the discomfort I was experiencing because I dismissed my feelings so quickly. It was as if they never existed. Something much more powerful and primal was at play within me, of which I had no awareness at the time. I participated actively in that joint meeting. In fact, I don't know if anyone spoke more vociferously against those *evil* directors than I, even though, in retrospect, I had little direct experience of their actions. Feelings were hurt, no compromise was reached, people suffered, and the two parties went their separate ways. A new organization was formed and has become successful, and the older organization recovered and it, too, is successful. I worked for two years at the new venture but became increasingly unhappy. My work suffered, and at the end of two years I resigned. The organization I left behind is thriving without me, and I'm happy about that because they do good work and their clients benefit from it. After a period of mourning and sadness, I went on to do some of the most gratifying work of my life, which I'm happy to say continues today. All's well that *is* well.

Over time, what came to light for me was that I had betrayed my true self because of a profound need to be included, part of, important to—something. Apparently, deep down I never felt I belonged. When one sits quietly in meditation, things come up, and sometimes what comes up are thoughts, feelings, and sensations we would rather not experience or acknowledge. Because we have an aversion to certain feelings, we go through life avoiding them or pushing them away. We busy ourselves frenetically with work, socializing, and the ongoing pursuit of more, bigger, better. We numb out in front of the TV to ensure that no quiet space exists in which our true feelings might be experienced.

By the time I was a teenager, I realized how much I felt like an outsider in my own home. I didn't share the values of dominant family members, and as a result, with the exception of a niece, I never became close with any of my family, even though there was an abundance of aunts, uncles, and cousins. My father often said to me, "You think you're better than we are." I didn't think that at all, I just had different interests and perspectives. I didn't have the intense interest in making large sums of money that my father so admired in my brother, and although I was too scared to ever say so, I never agreed with the violence my father used to discipline us. I'm sure the truth is that if I had wanted to be more involved with my family I could have, but feelings can muddle reality. They also have a major effect on decisions we make.

As I look back at that aforementioned meeting, I could have spoken up at any time and suggested that we put greater effort into negotiating, not separating. I could have pointed out that nothing positive could be accomplished by singling out those two directors. I could have drafted a proposal, a peaceful approach for us to try, but there was a strong pull inside or, perhaps more accurately, a deep fear that I would not be included if I suggested a different approach, if I didn't go along with the leadership. I believe the split would have happened anyway, but I would have been much happier had I been true to myself, my feelings, and my integrity.

Having come to that realization, about a year after that infamous meeting, I sought out the two directors and apologized to them for any actions on my part that might have caused them suffering. Both accepted my apology graciously, and both said, with tears in their eyes, how much my coming forward in that way meant to them. In that light, I have made it a point to be more closely in touch with my intentions. Examining the concept of karma is beyond the scope of this exploration, but the Buddha's teachings are clear in describing intention as the principal factor in determining the karmic imprint of a particular action.

POCKET PRACTICE

Work this sentence (or a similar one) into your conversations, especially when there is disagreement: "Let me think about that."

This simple statement can prevent us from making quick decisions that we might regret, or from speaking while angry, which we'll surely regret. It also sends a message that we care enough about the other person that we want to take time to consider what they've said. (In all fairness, I must admit that more than once my then teenage daughter demanded, "Why do you always have to think about it? You're a parent, you should just know.")

POCKET PRACTICE

Contemplate often questions such as, *In what situations am I most likely to stray from my values?*

Other questions to reflect on regularly (especially after being in disagreement with another): *Do I feel clean about my words and actions? Do I enjoy the Bliss of Blamelessness?* (The Bliss of Blamelessness is a state of mind described by the Buddha, which arises from not feeling guilty about anything we have said or done.) The fruit of this practice sometimes ripens slowly, and we may need time to see our own truth clearly. Be patient; the rewards will be there.

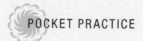
POCKET PRACTICE

Sit with your eyes closed and contemplate one of the five precepts described earlier.

Spend time with each one every day for a week and consider its potential benefit in your life.

This is best done by taking at least ten quiet minutes each day. Here are the precepts listed again:

- To refrain from killing or harming any living being (which includes tiny creatures)
- To refrain from taking anything that is not freely given (which includes small things, such as paper clips and rubber bands)
- To refrain from sexual misconduct (which includes with vulnerable people)
- To refrain from false, harmful, or harsh speech (which includes gossip)
- To refrain from abusing intoxicants (which includes anything that can keep you from thinking clearly)

POCKET PRACTICE

For a week, several times a day, as you are about to do something, anything, even the simplest act, ask yourself, *What is my intention?*

This may appear to be simple, but you'll find it invaluable as a tool, a reminder, to be in touch with your intentions. Try it for a few hours. For instance, you head for the refrigerator. As you touch the handle, the inner dialogue might go something like this:

What is my intention?

To get a bit of that delicious leftover rice pilaf.

Okay. What is my motivation?

It tastes good, and it gets me away from the computer for a few minutes.

Fair enough. Enjoy your snack.

POCKET PRACTICE

When you touch the phone, about to make a call or send a text message, ask yourself, *What is my intention?* As you are about to enter a meeting, ask yourself, *What is my intention?*

This is the logical follow-up to the previous exercise. Pick a day and practice many times throughout that day. No one will know you are doing it, and you may experience some real surprises.

When I do a whole week of this practice, which might include doing the exercise fifty or more times, I often get playful and create variations to keep my awareness sharp. Instead of a simple *What is your intention?* I might become a drill sergeant and shout (to myself), *IntenSHUN!* Or I become a sweet little old lady and ask myself in a crackly voice, *Young man, what is your intention?* If you do something like this, have fun but don't get so caught up in the playfulness that you lose sight of the purpose, which is to become intimately aware of your intentions *before* speaking or acting. Usually it takes very little time, yet every so often you might be startled at what you discover to be your intention. Then a different dimension opens. This is not a practice about words and actions but rather about the underlying processes that precede them—specifically, intentions. By becoming more mindful of your intentions, you are much more likely to think, speak, and act as the person you want to be—your *true self.* There is no moral judgment here. You make the decisions, but make those decisions in accordance with the person you want to be.

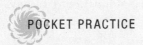 **POCKET PRACTICE**

Envision a person whose moral character you admire and

imagine that you are telling them of a decision you are about
to make.

This practice is like seeking the advice of a great
spiritual leader. You don't actually need a comment from
them; their very presence in your mind can be beneficial
and grounding. The inspiration of their spirit can help
you touch your true self.

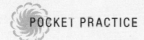 POCKET PRACTICE

Each day for two weeks, sincerely praise others' words or
deeds.

The key to this practice is sincerity. Since it may
be difficult to admire the actions of some, start with
people you like and work your way up to those you find
difficult. Eventually, you will be able to find something
worth praising in the actions of just about everyone. It
is a way to be in the world that benefits you and those
around you.

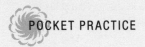

POCKET PRACTICE

Take time each day, every day, to practice being the person
you want to be.

This straightforward exercise can be penetrative
and transformative. Remember that in each moment of
conscious practice, you are being the person you want
to be.

3

Relinquishing

a home of twigs and chirps
the birds learn to fly, then soar
the nest stays behind
—MICHO

E xcept for one year when I lived in Southern California, and lots of touring and travel, I've lived my
entire life in New York City. I love the creative
energy and melting-pot atmosphere of people from all
over the world, and the endless array of performances,
markets, bookstores, street fairs, and museums. Most of
the time I can block out the noise, smile at the inefficien-
cies, avoid rush hour, and feel good about picking up
after my dog. By and large, unlike popular rumor, I find
Big Applers to be warm, helpful, and downright friendly.
Our apartment has the charm and character typical of a

prewar building and is spacious enough for Susanna, me, and our golden retriever, the Artful Dodger. I was convinced, as was Susanna, that I did not want the responsibilities and hassles of owning a house. Yet in the summer of 1994, we found ourselves shopping for a little weekend home. (We need never be bound by the limitations of our previous or current thinking, nor are we ever locked into being the person we used to be, or think we are.)

Susanna's one stipulation for her new home was that it had to be a house in which she would not hear outside traffic. I learned not to become interested in a particular house until she had placed her stethoscope to the ground in various strategic places throughout the property. If as much as a tricycle was in motion five miles away, she'd hear it and the house would be ruled out. Miraculously, after only two months of shopping and decibel checking, we made an offer for a gracious log home secluded in the woods of Litchfield County, Connecticut. On Thanksgiving Day, we sat on a mattress, the only piece of furniture that had been delivered, and ate a *Stop & Shop* holiday dinner in our new home. While lacking in certain family traditions and gastronomical delights, that Thanksgiving dinner had a flavor that neither of us has ever forgotten.

The next day, we walked up into the wooded acreage of our new property, fascinated by the variety of trees, plants, wildlife, insects, and mosses that inhabited the land. It seemed absolutely magical. There was, however, an underlying, subtle sense of . . . I wasn't sure what it was, perhaps disjointedness. As we walked, we slowly gained clarity. We had a piece of paper that named us as the owners of this property, yet surely there could be no such thing. How can anyone truly own trees, or part of the earth? We cannot own the animals, birds, insects, or worms on, above, or below the surface of "our property." The deed was a legal document necessary for social order, but beyond that, it seemed meaningless. The sense of something much greater than the law of the land was present. We decided in that moment that we were to be the caretakers of this parcel of land and the creatures that inhabited it. It would be our privilege to preserve its beauty and integrity and, when possible, gently enhance it.

Over time, the beautiful property seemed to become even more so. It retained its rustic in-the-woods quality while offering the comforts of a secluded retreat house. From Thursday evenings to Monday mornings we were country folk, planting a tree, building a table, fixing the occasional leak, and reading a book in front of the fireplace.

Then, ten years after buying the house, we founded the

Community of Peace and Spirituality in New York City, offering a spiritual gathering every Sunday morning. At that point our schedule changed dramatically. No longer could we officiate a Saturday-night wedding and go back to the house for a leisurely Sunday. It became more difficult to leave the city early on Thursdays, and, at best, we had to be back by late Saturday afternoon to be ready for the Community's Sunday-morning activities. By the time we had lived this hectic schedule for a year we found ourselves discussing the possibility of giving up the house. With a nod to the impermanent nature of all things, we made the decision to put the house on the market. The first people who looked at it loved it, and we accepted their offer.

The time we spent in the house before the transition was completed turned out to be remarkably rich and powerful. There was so much that we loved about the house, the property, and the lifestyle that we would be leaving behind. I saw details along the road as we drove to and from the house as I had never seen them before. I walked the gardens and the woods with a greater presence. I breathed in the fragrances and colors of the flowers, trees, and sky with greater awareness of their nuances. I looked at woodworking pieces that I had made, most of which would not fit in our New York home and would have to be sold or given away. I could feel in the memory of my hands the selection, measuring, cutting, joining, and finishing of the wood. I was living with the preciousness of my dwindling time with something I loved. Whatever sadness there was in my heart was brightened by the joy of the increased depth of awareness, the overwhelming richness of life when one is fully present to its vibrant energy. I was living in harmony with the absolute reality that my time with the sight, smell, touch, sound, and taste of this part of my life was coming to an end. Awareness of its impending death was enriching my life.

The end of our time living in Connecticut was by choice. We were not being forced to give up the house. At the same time, a metaphor was inescapable—one day, at a time not yet known to me, I will have to give up the *entire* house. As my dear wife says, "We all have to take the big trip." Every religion and spiritual path offers a view of the end of this life and what lies beyond. We can have great faith, yet it can be challenging to accept that we cannot actually know the answers to many of life's biggest questions. For some, it can be downright terrifying. As a society, we avoid the subject of death with an adamancy that suggests a belief that denial of reality can change its outcome. The danger is that denial of reality leaves one in ignorance, and ignorance is the fertile ground for fear, and fear obliterates freedom. Consider: the nature of reality is such that with or without our acceptance, recognition, or belief, it is.

Sometimes the fear of letting something go turns out to be greater than the actual relinquishment. When I was a boy I used to watch a television program on Sunday afternoons called *Omnibus*. It was the beginning of what would become the best of public television. I was highly influenced by a series of programs called *Young People's Concerts,* conducted and taught by Leonard Bernstein. My childhood was difficult; my mother died when I was a teenager, and my father suffered from a serious mental illness that made him abusive, uncommunicative, and often violent. It would be safe to say that I grew up in a state of constant underlying trepidation punctuated with frequent periods of outright terror. However, since it was all I knew, it must have felt all right—a kind of "I'm not okay, you're not okay, and that's okay" scenario.

Then this extraordinary music entered my life and I was transported. At the age of fifteen I made one of my first adultlike decisions and joined the RCA Victor Record Club. My membership began with recordings of all nine Beethoven symphonies conducted by Arturo

Toscanini—a fiery and brilliant musician—what a treasure. Each month I received another recording, including my first exposure to opera, *La Bohème*, also conducted by Toscanini. These were recordings of live performances, and the impassioned voice of Toscanini crying out with the singers was both thrilling and chilling. I was hooked, and I had also found my refuge. As each new recording arrived I would listen for hours (to the detriment of my schoolwork) and endlessly read the accompanying notes. Soon the monthly fix was not enough, and I began buying records with every penny I could scrape together from my little after-school jobs. Through the years the record collection grew ever larger, so that by the time I was in my thirties I had on my shelves well over two thousand vinyl discs. ("Vinyl discs"—that dates me, doesn't it?)

When I became an active professional singer I spent more time with live music and less time with recordings. The birth of my daughter, Samantha, brought the joys and responsibilities of fatherhood, and the time available for listening to music at home diminished even further. The joy of music never faded, but the nature of my beloved recordings began to shift from active use to that of a decorative presence. Then, some forty years after I began my record collection, I entered The New Seminary to study and become an Interfaith minister. Soon the shelves, comfortably filled with records, began to overflow as more and more books were added. A horizontal-space crisis, familiar to most New York City apartment dwellers, was rapidly developing, and a decision had to be made.

I felt a combination of anxiety and sorrow as I contacted record dealers and discussed a sale. I was also dismayed to learn how little my invaluable collection was worth on the market. In fact, the only reason an acceptable deal ultimately came about was that Susanna's set of complete *Beatles* recordings was deemed to be of extraordinary value. So it came to pass that on a sunny morning in July, a treasured part of my past, the solace of my early years, was boxed up in a few dozen used liquor cartons and hauled away in a quite ordinary-looking dark blue panel truck.

From time to time in the ensuing weeks I would notice a slight sense of loss, sadness, and regret. No matter, after weighing the particulars and acknowledging the impermanent nature of all things, the decision to sell the records had been made, and books of all sizes and shapes have been replacing them ever since. A small collection of CDs has proven sufficient for at-home listening.

Giving up the records was a great blessing. It presented an opportunity to experience, in a real way, the practice of relinquishing, of letting go, of enjoying things without becoming attached to them. This feeling of pleasure without attachment is akin to the experience of love without possessiveness or condition. It is this manner of love that is one of the greatest of human experiences, the sacred experience that inspires the highest spiritual and creative self. It is this love that has the potential to see through our differences and guide us on a path to a profoundly more meaningful life.

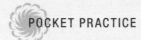 **POCKET PRACTICE**

At least once each year, go through your belongings, choose one that you really like, and designate it to be given away.

You might like to do this practice twice a year—it helps keep the home neater. What you give away need not be something whose absence would alter your lifestyle, nor should its disposal cause hardship for you or your family, but it should be significant to you—not that old relic you've been wanting to get rid of anyway. Give away something that you enjoy. Don't be concerned if you feel some reluctance. It doesn't mean you're greedy or selfish. Remember, ours is a society that encourages acquiring more. We rarely hear about the simple pleasures of having less. Our entire economic system, shaky though it has proven to be, is based on knowing that you and I can so easily be convinced that we absolutely must have the newest, fastest, most vastly improved model. Yet the practice of letting go of things can be invaluable. We become less possessive, less attached, less distressed at loss (such as the loss of a glove or a sock) or damage (such as a scratch on the fender). In turn for what we give away, we gain freedom and lightness. Perhaps more important, we prepare in a gentle way for that time when we must let go of everything—when we must leave behind everyone and everything we hold dear. We will have no choice; there are no exceptions. Try giving things away, but don't *waste* away a single precious moment. You never know, this may be the only life you get. The practice of letting go helps us heed the Buddha's advice: to prepare now for your salvation.

Looking directly at the ever-changing nature of all things is not necessarily easy, but until one fully accepts the reality of impermanence, including the impermanent nature of one's self, and can find some degree of comfort with its certainty, one cannot be truly free. I'm not at all certain that we've been offered much in the way of support from our Western religions. If we had, we might not experience such fear of aging and death. We might not support the enormous industries that attempt to convince us of the appeal of looking young as they bombard us with questionable products that hydrate our well-earned wrinkles and dehydrate our hard-earned funds. We might not so casually discard one of our greatest potential reservoirs of wisdom—our senior citizens. We might be more comfortable with silence, and more peaceful even as our fears and concerns arise. We might experience greater joy and appreciation for who we are and what we have. We might be better able to accept that along with the wondrous delights of life there are sorrows as well. We might be better able to maintain a sense of equanimity as we navigate the ocean of life—an ocean that comprises ten thousand joys and ten thousand sorrows.

A teaching of the Buddha called the Upajjhatthana Sutta (Subjects for Contemplation) is known for five compelling insights into the fragile nature of life and what is truly ours. It is wise to examine all aspects of reality, even those that at first may feel uncomfortable. Such exploration will, over time, dissolve fear and lead to wisdom and freedom.

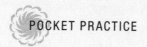 **POCKET PRACTICE**

Sit quietly and contemplate these five powerful insights.
Progress gradually, perhaps working with one contemplation
once a month.

- *I am of the nature to grow old; I cannot avoid aging.*
- *I am subject to illness; I cannot avoid illness.*
- *I am subject to death; I cannot avoid death.*
- *All that is dear to me and everyone I love are of the nature to change. I will be separated from all that is dear and loved by me. There is no way to escape being separated from them.*
- *I am the owner of my actions. My actions are my only true belongings. I cannot escape the consequences of my actions. My actions are the ground on which I stand.*

Find your own comfort level and be compassionate with yourself. These teachings are powerful and are often avoided because we think they are depressing or frightening; or we take an "I'll deal with these things when I must" attitude. If you are just beginning this type of practice, go slowly and go gently.

Our freedom exists entirely within ourselves. No one can release us; only we can do that. Often, in order to move toward our own happiness, we have to give up all interest in being right and showing others the error of their ways. Do you allow your happiness to depend on your being right?

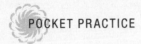

POCKET PRACTICE

Consider whether it's more important for you to be right or to be happy.

When we are in conflict with someone, it may be advantageous to let go of being right. Most of us like to be right and are willing to explain why we are. However, when the other person feels just as adamantly that they are right, discussions can easily become unpleasant. No matter how certain we are that we are right, there is always the possibility that we are not. Your acknowledging the possibility that you may not be right might serve as a hint to the other that they, too, might not be right. Oddly enough, there are times when neither party is right (or wrong). In any event, would you rather be right or be happy?

Sometimes what we have to let go of is our deep desire for things to be different, or to have been different—because they aren't, and they weren't. We might have to give up a subtle belief that because we were victimized, we are damaged and can never enjoy a meaningful relationship or a successful career. We might have to let someone else off the hook in order that we might be free. Each of us can examine our own thought processes and see if there is something we could give up in order to gain true freedom.

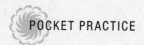

POCKET PRACTICE

Consider letting someone off the hook for a deed they committed or harsh words they spoke.

Look deeply within for any bitterness or residual anger that you may still harbor toward that person. Even when someone is long out of our lives or even deceased, we may be holding resentment toward them. Who is being hurt by those feelings? Resolve that it's time to let that negativity go. If you've been holding resentment for a long time, it may take a while to release it, but stay the course with gentle firmness. Ultimately, you will be able to take a deep breath and enjoy your new freedom. Remember, we cannot have a better past, but we can usually have a better present.

mentioned earlier that when I was on retreat with the Vietnamese Zen monk Thich Nhat Hanh, he commented that when Americans say they are hungry, it is usually because they skipped breakfast or arrived home late for dinner. From his perspective, as one who has worked with some of the poorest people on earth, there must be a certain irony to our "hunger." It is believed that the health benefits of fasting are far-ranging, and so for many it is practiced on a regular basis. In some traditions of Buddhism, monks and nuns do not eat after the noon meal, although this is not considered fasting but rather part of the discipline to support their meditation practice. One can gain deep insights through relinquishing food for even half a day. Experiencing the sensations of hunger and, in my case, the mild headache that often accompanies hunger have helped me be more comfortable with discomfort. It has also allowed me to feel, even if minimally, what so many of my fellow beings around the world experience each day. This type of experience opens the door to true compassion.

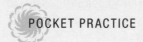

POCKET PRACTICE

Once a month for six months, do not eat for half a day.

Try not eating until three or four in the afternoon or, if it works better in your schedule, don't eat anything after lunch. If this would be difficult during the week, try it on the weekend. The object is not to torture yourself but to open to greater awareness.

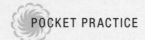

POCKET PRACTICE

Recite the five contemplations below before each meal.

This practice also comes from my days in the Thich Nhat Hanh community. Reciting these five contemplations helps bring awareness to the gift of food and our relationship to it. Eating is a joyful activity in which we are fortunate to partake. That is not the case in much of the world. Try saying the contemplations to yourself if you are eating alone, or sharing them with others just before you begin a meal. You may find people thanking you.

> This food is the gift of the whole universe—the earth, the
> sky, and much loving work.
> May we eat mindfully and be grateful to receive this food.
> May we eat with moderation.
> May we eat foods that promote health and prevent illness.
> May this food nourish us along the path of understanding
> and love.

4

Wisdom

east moon elevates
the west embraces the sun
between them our path
—MICHO

Wat would it be like to consistently enjoy the ease of clear, insightful thinking? What would it be like to feel calm and to make intelligent decisions in stressful situations? The quality that supports this kind of experience is called wisdom. In the Buddhist tradition the development of wisdom is said to arise from the ability to see things as they really are, not as they appear to be. We can think of this type of discriminative awareness as a state of mindfulness in which one is fully present, lucid, and free from the consequences brought about by habitual responsive patterns and knee-jerk reactions. Here is a beautiful example of seeing things as they really are: during World War II, when housing was in short supply, a kindly lady said to a five-year-old, "I'm sorry your family doesn't have a home." The child answered, "Oh, we have a home. We just don't have a house to put it in."

Wisdom is not learned from books or teachers, valuable though they may be. Wisdom is learned through personal experience, which is why we tend to associate it with older people—those who have been around longer and had more life experiences. However, I've met a few people who exhibited signs of wisdom at an early age, and I've certainly known some old fools. Unfortunately, wisdom is often attained only after paying a hefty price. Confucius said, "By three methods we may learn wisdom: first, by reflection, which is the noblest; second, by imitation, which is the easiest; and third, by experience, which is the bitterest."

One can have extensive knowledge, success, power, and influence without attaining wisdom. Not so many years ago we witnessed an American president, intelligent enough to earn a prestigious Rhodes Scholarship, display such a serious lack of wisdom in his personal life that his scandalous activity led to embarrassment for himself, his family, and his country, and ultimately to Congress initiating impeachment proceedings against him. More recently, another highly intelligent man, a governor of New York, was forced to resign due to the same type of obsessive behavior. In the aftermath of September 11, 2001, yet another president declared that responsibility for the tragic events of that day lay directly with "the evil one," presumably Osama bin Laden, and that Mr. Bin Laden and his evil cohorts must be hunted down and killed. Somehow, the president ultimately concluded that the wisest course of action was, therefore, to declare war on Iraq. Without getting into the politics involved in these situations, the decisions made would appear to be severely lacking in wisdom. The president's decision to enter into a war cost thousands of lives and an enormous amount of suffering. Billions of dollars were spent to facilitate the war, money that surely could have gone to better use. Make no mistake, there are times when it is advisable to take action in order to stop oppression, cruelty, and injustice. Such action, whether on an individual or global level, requires great wisdom and compassion, two traits sorely lacking in many of our political leaders. Without wisdom and compassion, we only trade one version of cruelty and injustice for another, and, invariably, many suffer while we make the transition. Understanding that there are always consequences to our actions is at the very heart of wisdom.

Wisdom enables us to see beyond ego and to gain clarity where there might otherwise be confusion. Wisdom is free from greed, hatred, and delusion. Wisdom sees that taking the same action over and over again and expecting the results to be different is a form of insanity. Through the eyes of wisdom we look at history and see that if war was the way to peace, we would have had a world at peace a very long time ago. We have tried war time and again through the millennia, and we still do not live in a world at peace. We can look at our personal history the same way. When we have been in conflict with others, has it brought inner peace? Wisdom invites us to explore other ways when our current approach is not working. Wisdom asks us to consider what the Buddha referred to as the Eternal Law: "Hatred does not cease by hatred, by love alone does hatred cease" (Dhammapada 5). How different the world would be today if, on September 12, 2001, our leaders had sat down and explored such questions as: Have we played a role in this tragedy? How can we move toward peace rather than war? How can we end this hatred? It almost seems like naive thinking, yet it is exactly the path followed by those whom we have most admired, exalted, and revered throughout history—people like Mohandas Gandhi, Aung San Suu

Kyi, His Holiness The Dalai Lama, and the Reverend Martin Luther King Jr.

On a personal level, wisdom invites us to look deeply at situations in our own lives that are not working as well as we would like—perhaps a relationship or career—and to explore how we might be undermining our happiness. Most of us tend to look at the people and conditions outside ourselves to provide our happiness. Yet the reality is that if we cannot find happiness within ourselves, we cannot find happiness anywhere. Our quality of life is determined not by the people and events in our lives but by how we experience those people and events. All that we are is the result of our thoughts—with our thoughts, we make our world.

Albert Einstein, a wise man indeed, taught that each of us is part of an entity that we call the universe. We experience ourselves—our thoughts, perceptions, and feelings—as something separate from everything and everyone else. He called this a kind of "optical delusion of consciousness." In this state of delusion, a state in which we experience ourselves as the center of the universe, we imprison ourselves, which restricts us from seeing beyond our own wants and desires and from caring for more than a few beings close to us whom we find appealing and worthy. Einstein said that the way to free ourselves from this imprisonment is to learn to care about other beings—in fact, all beings and all of nature.

The Buddha taught that all phenomena arise due to the causes and conditions that precede and accompany them. In other words, all events, all feelings, all situations are born, and likewise pass away, due to the concurrence of accompanying factors. Nothing exists by itself; everything exists in relation to everything else. If we plant a rosebush, there must be sufficient sunlight, moisture, and nutrients if the plant is to flourish and produce flowers. Without the proper conditions coming together, the plant withers. This concept applies to all things. Understanding and accepting the interdependent nature of all things lays the ground-work for the arising of wisdom. It is a vital element in seeing things as they really are. It is also wise to remember that it is the nature of a rosebush to produce roses. If we want lilies to appear, we will be disappointed. It is basic wisdom as found in the hit musical *The Fantasticks*: "Plant a carrot, / get a carrot, / not a brussels sprout." How often are we hurt when a friend or relative reacts in the same way he always has and not in the way we would want? Even though we might have a preference for lilies, allowing ourselves the spaciousness to take in the unique qualities of roses is not only wise, it can alleviate suffering.

The death of my mother when I was a teenager and the illness and brutality of my father would not have been on my youthful wish list. But suffering relates to wanting things to be different from the way they are or, perhaps, different from the way they were. Things *are* the way they are, and things *were* the way they were, and, like you, I'm still here navigating the enormous cerulean ocean of life and basking in the brilliant sunshine of this very moment. To experience suffering and not emerge as a person of greater compassion, love, and generosity would seem a waste. Identifying the cause of our suffering and setting about on a course to alleviate it is walking the path of wisdom. That effort will be well rewarded.

My friend Natalie is a genuinely kind person with a sincere interest in others, a smile for everyone, a creative mind, and a sweet, joyful demeanor. Even when she was dealing with life's hassles she could see the brighter side, and it was always fun to be with her. How could she, or any of us, have imagined the horror that would suddenly change the course of her life? That horror struck on the morning of September 11, 2001, when her husband, Timothy, her love since childhood and the father of their five-year-old, was trapped in the World Trade Center. Just before he died, Timothy reached Natalie on his cell phone, and their final conversation was surreal and unbearable. She couldn't believe what she was hearing. In an instant, her world, her beautiful, perfect world, crumbled.

During the next year, Natalie's sparkling eyes were the color of tears and her resolve was severely tested, but I never heard anger or hatred in her voice. Her heart, though shattered, remained gentle and caring. She spoke often of the tremendous love and support being offered to her by family, friends, and strangers from all over the world. She shared her feelings openly, speaking of her sadness and grief but never of anger or hatred toward those who had killed Timothy. She said that hatred wouldn't accomplish anything but to cause more misery for herself and those around her. She only hoped and prayed that the world would someday come to its senses. I told her that she was practically quoting the Buddha, who said, "Hatred does not cease by hatred; by love alone does hatred cease." She agreed and thought the old guy was pretty wise. A few years later, to the delight of her family and friends, Natalie met and married Paul, whom, she believed, Timothy had sent to her.

Surely Natalie's open, loving heart was a major factor in her healing and her ability to again find happiness. Not being burdened by clinging to anger, resentment, and bitterness can make bearable the journey through life's most challenging times and leaves us open to moments of peace and grace along the way. Holding on to negative feelings hardens the heart and closes us off from the happiness that can be ours, even during difficult times. When we hold on to anger because of what we feel another person has done, we are not being wise. When we allow ourselves to become bitter because we are in a difficult situation that we feel can never change, we are again not being wise. However, when we see that any situation can, and will, change, we are seeing things as they really are, and that is the ground of wisdom. It is also wise to do what we can to encourage the change within ourselves that will free us from anger, resentment, and bitterness. As mentioned previously, it is not situations and conditions that cause our happiness and unhappiness but how we experience those situations. When we see this clearly we can think, speak, and act in ways that relieve sorrow and misery and lead to greater happiness for ourselves and those around us.

People say that our world is violent. If we are to do anything about that, we need to address our own feelings of suspicion, resentment, anger, and hostility toward individuals or groups of people. Sometimes we may feel we can solve a problem quickly with aggressive action and adamancy, but such solutions are often achieved at the expense of the rights or dignity of others. One problem may be solved, but another is created, thus continuing the cycle of disruption. On a global level we can see clearly how total victory for one side and total defeat for the other is not possible, and certainly not sustainable. So it is, as well, with our personal relationships. When we are in conflict, the only wise solution will come from compassionate thoughts, words, and actions. Those actions may be firm, but they must also be kind.

One doesn't have to be religious to lead a moral life or to attain wisdom. Whether one is a believer or a nonbeliever, what matters is that we have a genuine sense of caring for one another. That concern for the welfare of others emerges naturally when we see the interconnected nature of all beings. As the Dalai Lama has pointed out, we live on a small and fragile planet. Amid our perceived differences, we tend to forget how the world's various religions, ideologies, and political systems were meant to serve beings, not destroy them. For wisdom to arise we must commit ourselves to living peacefully, truthfully, with kindness, generosity, and compassion. We must *be* in the world from that perspective.

Near the end of the Buddha's life, his attendant Ananda asked who would be their teacher when the

Buddha passed away. The Buddha replied that each person must be a lamp unto themselves, meaning that each of us must learn to see the true nature of things. That is the essence of wisdom—to see and understand for ourselves how things really are. The development of wisdom requires an open mind and the ability to listen to views that are different from our own, to be objective rather than knowing, and to be open to changing our views when truth contradicts them. This skillful way of living is often referred to as "Beginner's Mind."

Years ago, as a young man at the beginning of my career as a professional singer, I was in the original Broadway company of *Oliver!* There was a scene at the end of the first act in which Oliver picks the pocket of Mr. Brownlow. The whole cast becomes involved in a wild chase, trying to catch the elusive little thief. One night, about two years into the Broadway run, I came zipping across the stage chasing Oliver, only to find the entire rest of the cast pulling a prank on me by running in the wrong direction. I tried to act cool and go along with the joke, while at the same time thinking that they were not acting very professionally in front of a sold-out Broadway house. When the curtain came down my colleagues remained onstage, looking at me with vague, inquisitive smiles, the same way I must have been looking at them. The stage manager approached me tentatively and asked if I was all right, and I assured him that I was. "Well, then," he barked, "what the hell were you doing?" Apparently, in a moment of complete mindlessness, I had left out an entire section of staging, resulting in everyone else being in the *wrong place*. It took me several days to fully accept that *I* was the one who was in the wrong place. Since then I have often wondered if humanity divides itself naturally into those who, when there is disagreement, immediately assume they are right and those who, just as reactively, immediately assume they are wrong. Either way, we leave out the process of evaluating the information before us and risk not making wise decisions. In this instance, I certainly did not see things as they really were.

After *Oliver!* I was in another show on Broadway called *Pickwick*. There was a song in that show called "If I Ruled the World." (Too bad it was the only popular song—I was out of work in six months.) In this song, Pickwick sings that if he ruled the world, everything would be perfect; everyone would have everything they could possibly want. He declared that if he ruled the world, "Every head would be held up high / there'd be sunshine in everyone's sky." Audiences cheered every night, but the trouble is, that is not reality. Human existence comprises both joys and sorrows. That is reality, and it is that very reality that affords us an ever-evolving opportunity for growth, wisdom, and enlightenment

We live in the Information Age and greatly value knowledge. Unfortunately, our desire to accrue knowledge can blind us to its greatest potential—the development of wisdom. Consider the successful businessman who heard about a wise master in a neighboring town. He requested a visit, and when he arrived he introduced himself to the master as one who had created a number of successful businesses and was quite wealthy. He was married to a beautiful woman, and his children were doing well in their chosen professions. He was a moral person who gave to the poor and was highly respected in his community. "I'm an intelligent man with much experience in life," he said, "yet I'm sure I could learn something from a great teacher like you." The master replied, "Let us consider how we might go about this while we enjoy a cup of tea together." The master placed a cup before his guest and began to pour the tea. As the cup filled, the master continued to pour and it overflowed, spilling on the businessman's expensive clothing. "Stop! Are you crazy? Can't you see the cup is full and there's no room for any more?" The master replied, "Ah, yes, I can see that, but can you see that you are so full with all that you know that there is no room for anything more?"

Ah, Beginner's Mind—it knows nothing; how peaceful, how wise.

Not long ago I was on a ten-day retreat studying the nature of mind with the delightful young Tibetan teacher Yongey Mingyur Rinpoche. Early one morning, while sitting in the bathroom (pardon the specific, but it illustrates how strange feelings can arise at any time), I was suddenly overcome by a powerful fear of claustrophobia. That might sound redundant, "fear of claustrophobia," since claustrophobia is itself a fear, but since I was not actually experiencing claustrophobia, it was more a fear of the fear itself. Nothing like this had ever happened to me before, and I had never actually experienced claustrophobia, but retreats can bring up all sorts of things, and this was certainly a classic example. Months before, Susanna and I had been planning a trip to Africa, which, because of where we would be going, required booking far in advance. The plans were complete, and it was still a year before the safari was to take place. The travel from camp to camp would be done by small aircraft with a seating capacity of eight or fewer, and there would be several such flights of one to two hours each. In my previous travels I have flown in planes barely capable of holding four cramped passengers and never experienced any problems, so this fear came as a complete surprise. In my claustrophobic vision, the details of the planes were precise and clear. The interior was all shiny white plastic with tiny windows and no larger than a fist and not enough headroom to stand up. In truth, I have never seen such a plane, and probably no one else has, either. No matter, it was there in my mind and the claustrophobic feeling was frightening. The intensity of discomfort was so overwhelming, I felt in that moment that I had absolutely no choice but to cancel the trip. It all happened in a matter of seconds—fear can come upon us so quickly. Then, calling on years of practice, I calmed myself and thought, *Wait, this is just a feeling. There is no reality to this other than experiencing a feeling. There is no such plane, and there is no claustrophobia. You, my friend, are completely safe.* The fear subsided rather quickly, but for several minutes my pounding heart continued to bear witness to the fact that I had gone through a real experience. The feeling was real, the plane was not. To learn more about this phenomenon, and to assure myself that I would be calm when the actual travel was at hand, I re-created the situation in my next meditation session and was able to conjure up the fear again, although not on as intense a level. Over the next couple of weeks, I created the situation in my meditation a few more times until there was no more fear.

Understanding that our thoughts, feelings, and sensations are not reality is essential to the arising of wisdom.

They are real thoughts, feelings, and sensations but not reality. They may be incredibly intense, but they are still just feelings. This insight can help us think, speak, and act more wisely. As an example, the safari turned out to be fantastic, and canceling it because of an ungrounded fear would have been unfortunate, not to mention foolish.

When we don't see things clearly, we can easily become overwhelmed by fear. The Buddha told a story of a man who went to his barn at dusk, and in the pale light he suddenly saw a snake coiled directly in front of him. His heart began to pound wildly, his palms became sweaty, and on wobbly legs he backed away and ran into his house only to spend a sleepless night. The next day, when the sun was up full, he cautiously returned to the barn to see if the dangerous creature was still there. Instead, he found the serpent that had so frightened him in the dim light was actually a coiled rope. The light of day allowed him to see the truth, and he was greatly relieved.

When I first worked with my teacher Sharon Salzberg, I would often tell her about something that had come to me in meditation or that I had come to understand through studying the Buddha's teachings. She would listen attentively and say something like, "Yes, that's wonderful." Then she would often add, "Of course, it depends," and she would offer other possible views of my insights. After I heard "It depends" a number of times, I began to realize that things just aren't always as matter-of-fact, clear-cut, and certain as they appear to be. Sharon was praising my efforts and, at the same time, encouraging me to explore all possibilities.

The development of wisdom, for most of us, is a long process, so we will look at several Pocket Practices that can be used one at a time, or in conjunction with one another. You are wise—use these practices wisely.

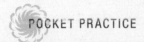 POCKET PRACTICE

On a regular basis, choose a particular situation and practice Beginner's Mind.

The essential characteristic of Beginner's Mind is openness—the willingness to explore all possibilities. The brain does not have a delete button, and it is naive, not to mention unrealistic, to try to disregard all we have learned. Beginner's Mind sees past what it knows and openly embraces all possibilities. The expert sees no advantage to such an approach;

he has it all figured out. For him there is nothing more to learn about the subject. Those with Beginner's Mind are curious, free of preconceptions, and able to enjoy the wonder and exploration of life. Release what you know and, like a wide-eyed child, take it all in anew. This allows room for insight and growth, and a wiser use of knowledge.

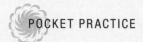

POCKET PRACTICE

Consider how your discomfort with a particular situation
might be eased by accepting things as they are.

Suffering usually relates to wanting things to be different from the way they are. Sit quietly, close your eyes, and open the spaciousness of mind and heart needed for a change of perspective. Remind yourself that even if a particularly difficult situation you are now confronting seems insurmountable, it is not fixed and solid. It will change. If after contemplating in this way for a few sessions you conclude that the situation is unacceptable, you should be better able to explore your options in a calmer and more compassionate manner.

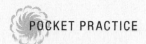

POCKET PRACTICE

Each evening for two weeks, recall one conversation you
had or one action you took during the day. Consider the
many possibilities that might result from your words or that
action.

There is no assumption in this practice that your
words or actions were skillful or unskillful. We simply want to increase our awareness that all our words
and all our actions have consequences. Some evenings
you will likely feel pleased doing this exercise. Other
times, perhaps not. Either way, you will be increasing
awareness.

POCKET PRACTICE

When the words or actions of another elicit anger within
you, stop before reacting and ask yourself, *Am I about to
speak and act as the person I want to be?*

Even the wisest among us can become angry, but the wise wait to speak or act until the fires have cooled. Do nothing until you have asked yourself if you are about to respond as the person you want to be. Take your time. If you look deeply, you'll have your answer. Then speak or act accordingly.

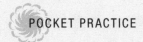 POCKET PRACTICE

Spend time with older folks; they're experienced at doing life.

Being a senior doesn't automatically make one wise, but the wise and the foolish alike have things to teach us. Don't judge whether or not you think they are smart. They've been at this business of life a long time, and that's good enough. Sit with them and listen. If you're fortunate enough to have living grandparents or parents, that's a great place to start. Otherwise, muster your courage and introduce yourself to a stranger. Older folks are often lonely because we, in our lack of wisdom, discard this most valuable resource, the wisdom of our seniors.

5

Joyous Effort

squawking geese at dusk
in seemingly aimless flight
my what's all the fuss
—MICHO

Tony just left. He was here tuning our piano, which
he has done twice a year ever since I can remember.
It's always a pleasure to have Tony in our home.
He's cheerful and funny, and at the slightest instigation
will let out a raucously loud laugh that resonates in the
piano and engulfs everyone within earshot. Whenever I
greet him and ask how he is, he always answers, "Pretty
good; I've stopped complaining." Then he lets out one of
those ear-shattering laughs. Tony is an excellent piano
tuner who, because he is blind, went through special
training in order to practice his profession. Six days a

week he maneuvers his way around New York City, which is not that easy for anyone, and tunes pianos for the most discriminating musicians. I can't imagine the effort that goes into doing all that Tony does, but I know it never appears effortful. He's pleased when he finishes with the piano and insists that I try it out. He grins broadly as I fumble through a few scales and arpeggios, either amused by my ineptitude or proud of his own tuning skill—which one I've never been able to tell. I do know that Tony has helped me understand the concept of "joyous effort" in a whole new light.

Rarely has anything significant been accomplished without effort. We can sometimes be fooled because people who are truly skillful often seem to function effortlessly. Great athletes would be an example, as would spiritually advanced individuals, since they often appear to navigate life with ease. However, in most cases a great deal of effort has preceded, and often accompanies, what appears to be effortlessness. Usually, such people have found reward in the effort itself. We know what that is like. Think about how much effort we joyfully expend when working at something we love to do. We put out an enormous amount of energy, and yet it can feel pleasurable, gratifying, and uplifting, like a great blessing. I would sometimes disappear into the workshop at our house for a woodworking project and not be seen again for days except for M-and-M's (meals and meditation). When my friend Linda works in her garden, every little baby plant is weeded, mulched, and fed before she comes inside. She might look muddy and weary, but she is uplifted by her experience in nature and ready for more the next day.

When I was directing in the theater, it was exhilarating for me to rehearse all day and then work through the night preparing for the next day's rehearsal. In the early '70s I was invited by Equity Library Theatre in New York City to direct an old melodrama from 1867 called *Under the Gaslight*. This was the first play in which someone was tied to the railroad tracks, and it was just filled with theatrical delights and challenges. The printed stage directions suggested that when the poor victim is tied down by the villain (boo, hiss) the sound of a train is heard in the distance coming from stage right (that's your left as you face the stage). Then the beam of the train's headlight would slowly start illuminating the stage as the "train" approached. After studying these directions for several days, a vision began to dance in my mind, one that I realized might end up as only a fantasy, considering our modest facility and limited budget. But the fantasy began taking shape in my mind; I had a vision, and I was somehow going to make it work. (My Buddhist friends might point out that I became attached to an idea, which is usually not wise. But I was young.) I began plotting the illusion of a train that would appear from the back of the stage, travel directly toward the audience, and go roaring right through the theater and out the back of the house. Needless to say, when I presented this proposal at the first production meeting, it was greeted with a unanimous and dismissive "Forget about it!" Actually, being in New York, it was probably more like "Fuhgeddaboutit!" In any event, that response was the inspiration this brash kid needed to go forward.

I wanted to work out all the details before involving the crew in rehearsal. They would have to be convinced that it could work and that the results would be well worth their efforts. We began by borrowing every set of portable speakers from anyone who would lend them to us. We wired them, starting with the smallest at the back of the stage and increasing in size all the way into and through the theater, and then decreasing in size out into the lobby. In all, I think we used about twenty sets of speakers. At the back of the stage, we mounted an ellipsoidal lamp (a standard stage light) on a stand that could be slowly turned and cranked higher and lower.

We covered it in black drapery so it would not be seen, except for the lens itself, which peeked through the drapery. The light, equipped with an adjustable iris that could open and close, was wired to a dimmer so its intensity could be increased as the "train" drew closer and closer. The concept was quite simple: The sound of the train's whistle would be heard far in the distance from the back of the dimly lit stage. Through the small opening in the back curtain, a faint light would be seen slowly turning into view, as if coming around a bend in the far-off distance. The sound of the train itself would now be heard in the distance, and the characters onstage—the good guy tied to the tracks and the leading lady who would soon turn heroine—suddenly would become aware of the imminent danger. The train light became brighter as the sound of the approaching train drew ominously closer—this being done by slowly increasing the volume and rolling the sound track from the back speakers to the front. Now the light, vibrating from the "movement of the train," was rushing closer at a frightening speed as the crescendoing sound was beginning to vibrate through the entire theater. The heroine dives onto the track, tears the lad's ropes loose, and pulls him out of harm's way, just barely escaping the roaring, massive vehicle. The sound of the train thunders at a deafening level into the theater as the lights clatter incessantly, flashing in our eyes and all around us. Finally, as the lights pass, the sound of the train fades into the distance. Virtue is triumphant.

There is a saying in the Zen tradition, "It is all quite simple—getting there is not always easy." The five dedicated men and women who stayed late every night for two weeks, working out the details and rehearsing the demands of the delicate coordination, were rewarded on opening night. As the train roared into the house, the audience jumped to their feet and cheered. They cheered for the good guy, they cheered for the heroine, they cheered for the triumph of good over evil. Maybe they just cheered to be part of the fun, I'm not really sure. I do know that my eyes were teary, my heart was pounding, and my body was trembling. All I could do was lean against the back wall of the theater and try to breathe.

Through the years, I have discussed various aspects of religion and spirituality with leaders from a number of traditions. I have found that while their approaches and specific beliefs may vary, they all seem to agree on one point—spiritual practice is not easy and requires effort, often heroic effort. The Sanskrit word for such effort is *viriya*, which essentially means determined perseverance in the face of whatever difficulties may arise. The Buddha taught that not only did one want to develop the quality of viriya, but that such heroic effort needed to be ethically intentioned as well. Concentrated effort directed toward an immoral act or greedy scheme could ultimately cause suffering and is not in the spirit of the virtuous quality of viriya. Thus, viriya is about great effort that is ethically motivated and skillfully directed.

We can bring the kind of effort to all of life that we bring to the activities we enjoy most. It doesn't mean that we will love all endeavors equally, but it does mean that we can derive pleasure from, or at least graciously accept, things that we previously experienced as annoying, boring, or distasteful. Overcoming aversion and fear is a major part of advancing spiritually. We overcome what the Buddha called "fetters" and "hindrances." To prevail in even the smallest bouts with laziness, greed, anger, ignorance, and negative thinking is a triumph. The effort required is not so much about trying to change as it is about becoming more aware of our thoughts, words, and actions in every moment. It is this increased awareness that facilitates change. We train the mind so that we can enjoy greater peace, happiness, wisdom, and equanimity.

Heroic effort is often needed when we decide to face head-on an area of our lives that is not working well, when we are ready to accept that the source of our unhappiness is within ourselves. We recognize that if things are going to change, we will have to put in effort—perhaps viriya, heroic effort. We begin by letting go of the belief that something or someone outside of ourselves is the cause of our unhappiness, and with well-directed effort we begin to see the situation as it really is. This can be messy work and can test our resolve. A number of years ago the primary relationship I had been in for more than a decade came to an end. I experienced a great deal of suffering as I began to accept that the source of my unhappiness was within myself. With guidance and great effort I began to see things as they really were. I saw that in my adult life I had never been just Allan. I had always been Allan and *someone*; I had never developed a most important relationship—the relationship with myself. It took real effort to learn to be by myself and feel whole. I practiced social seclusion for almost a year, which at first left me feeling undesirable, unattractive, and old. Gradually, the need to be with someone else faded and a greater appreciation of life developed. I, by myself, was enough. I came to realize how truly blessed I was. Out of that developed a more complete me, a person who could be in a healthy, equal, meaningful relationship if that was my choice. It was, and I believe I would not be in the beautiful relationship I enjoy today had I not put out the considerable effort needed to get to know me. We are responsible for our own happiness; it does not come from someone or something outside of ourselves. Our happiness can be enhanced by others, but we are the primary source.

Suppose we see ourselves as skillful at our chosen profession, but we do not have the career we feel corresponds to our capabilities. It is easy to blame external circumstances, but unless we are willing and courageous enough to put forth the effort to look deeply within, advancement is not likely to happen on its own. Likewise, if we believe the world is cheating us by not appreciating our talents and skills, that lack of appreciation is likely to continue. The work of looking within and recognizing the changes we need to make requires effort—and it may not be a smooth ride. Again, heroic effort may be necessary. This reminds me of the woman who was applying for a job at a large company. When the human resources director said to her, "You seem to be asking for a rather high salary for someone with no experience," the woman replied, "Well, yeah, the work is much harder when you don't know what you're doing."

My friend Ralph was program director at the Wisconsin Union Theater in Madison. In that capacity, he got to know many of the world's great artists. One night Luciano Pavarotti sang a recital at the theater. At the end the audience went wild, shouting "Bravo," throwing flowers, demanding encores, all in a tumultuous, rapturous outpouring of loving appreciation. Ralph told me he had never seen anything like it. Later, at dinner, he asked the great tenor what it felt like to receive such adulation. Pavarotti replied quietly, "It's a-nice." Then he explained that while he was happy to be appreciated, what mattered to him most was how he connected to the music when he sang. If he felt he had put out full effort toward that end, he was pleased. The audience was important, but his pleasure was not determined by others.

In one way or another, most of us need the approval of someone if we are to earn our livelihood. Whether they come to our garage to have their car fixed or to our office to have their broken leg fixed, it is usually necessary for people to like our work. However, we are much more likely to do well and feel successful if our efforts go into the task at hand rather than trying to win approval. Caring about all beings is loving and kind; trying to please all beings rarely works and is therefore unwise.

Learning to give full effort to our endeavors without

being attached to an outcome is one of the keys to happiness. What a revelation it can be when we realize how caught up we are in results and ego. "Will I succeed? What will Jim/Sue/Dad think of me if I don't?" There can be an enormous weight lifted from our shoulders when we learn to work giving full effort but releasing ourselves from attachment to results. We have surprisingly little control over the world around us, but we do have control over our perception of things. That's where we want to focus our efforts, because it is in our perceptions that the world becomes either harsh, unfriendly, and fearful or loving, joyful, and peaceful.

We can learn to give full effort and enjoy our endeavors without being attached to results. But it can be difficult to accept that results are rarely, if ever, in our hands. The actor puts full effort into an audition, yet the casting is not in his control. The student works diligently on an essay, but the grade is determined by the teacher. We make a magnificent sales pitch, but the purchasing decision is made by another. If we give full, joyful effort to our endeavors, then no matter what the result, we can feel good about ourselves. If we need to develop greater skills, we can do that with full effort as well.

Studies with senior citizens show that those who really went after what they wanted in life, even if they didn't get the outcome they desired, felt good about themselves, while those who said that they never really gave their full effort felt despondent and empty, as if they had wasted their lives. The Pocket Practices that cultivate determined effort have two main purposes. First, we can come to experience deeper levels of our physical, mental, and emotional resources that may have been previously untapped. This can be enormously satisfying and uplifting. Second, we become more skillful at addressing specific issues that may be causing us disappointment or distress.

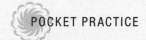 **POCKET PRACTICE**

> Once a week, push yourself to do one more repetition or to go five minutes longer on the treadmill than you would ordinarily.

Dig it out, grunt if necessary, then grin and enjoy the victory. Of course, this is for those who are doing some sort of physical workout. For those who are not, may this inspire you to start. Training the mind and training the body go well together.

POCKET PRACTICE

Spend a few quiet moments at the end of each day
considering and encouraging your most positive way of
thinking.

Support the type of thinking that leads you to feeling good, peaceful, and happy. Alternatively, discourage
negative patterns of thinking, such as when you start
creating scenarios in the mind that lead to negative or
depressing feelings. Notice how the mind almost seems to
have a mind of its own. It doesn't; you're in charge.

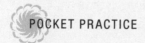

POCKET PRACTICE

Create a personal one-hour-and-twenty-minute retreat.

The schedule suggested here is intended as a guide,
so feel free to modify it to what suits you best, but once
you've created a schedule, stick to it for the full time.
The effort to do so is an essential part of the exercise.

The other essential element is that every moment during your retreat be spent with the intention of practicing awareness. The night before, prepare a special space for your retreat, perhaps adding a flower, a candle, incense, or whatever feels inspiring or uplifting. In the morning, wake up earlier than usual to let the body know that today will begin in a special way. Turn off the phone. Sit on a chair, a cushion, or whatever will be comfortable enough for you to be still for about ten minutes at a time.

6:00 a.m. Wake up; drink water if you wish but no coffee or breakfast yet. Brush your teeth and wash your face.

6:30 a.m. Sit quietly with your eyes closed or, if you prefer having your eyes open, take a soft focus at the floor about six feet in front of you. Bring your awareness to the sensations of your breath, noting the movement of air in and out at the nostrils or, if it is easier to observe, the gentle expansion and contraction of the abdomen.

6:40 a.m. Walk very slowly in a place where you can take ten to fifteen steps in each direction. Focus your attention on the movements of your legs and feet as you walk. Walk slowly and naturally, just observing the movements.

6:50 a.m.   Sit quietly, read a short inspirational piece or sacred text of your choosing, and consider how the teaching might be of benefit to you.

7:00 a.m.   Again, sit quietly with your eyes closed or, if you prefer having your eyes open, take a soft focus at the floor about six feet in front of you. Bring your awareness to the sensations of your breath, noting the movement of air in and out at the nostrils or, if it is easier to observe, the gentle expansion and contraction of the abdomen.

7:10 a.m.   Again, walk very slowly in a place where you can take ten to fifteen steps in each direction. Focus your attention on the movements of your legs and feet as you walk. Walk slowly and naturally, just observing the movements.

7:20 a.m.   Eat a light breakfast, perhaps a piece of fruit, a dish of yogurt, or a piece of toast. Chew very slowly, and allow your awareness to rest on the taste, aromas, and texture of each bite.

As you move into the rest of your day, do so with the same awareness you practiced while doing the exercises above.

If you enjoy this practice, do it once a month or even once a week. Slowly lengthen the times of the sitting and walking meditations to twenty or thirty minutes each. When you feel ready, you might want to consider spending a full day in retreat with others at a local meditation center. You can also spend a weekend or longer at a residential retreat center, such as Insight Meditation Society in Barre, Massachusetts, or Spirit Rock Meditation Center in Woodacre, California. There are many others in the United States and Europe, and throughout the world from which you can choose. The food is usually delicious, and the experience can be transformative.

To balance things out, let's look at a shorter, but very effective, practice. Often when we have to do something that is new for us and it doesn't come easily, we can become frustrated, annoyed, and anxious; we want to quit. When a new venture seems likely to test our intellect, resolve, or courage, we're often tempted to back away in order to protect our self-image and not damage our delicate ego. There is actually a better approach.

POCKET PRACTICE

Focus on effort, not results. When facing new and challenging situations, projects, or adventures, take a few moments throughout the day and remind yourself, *I can do this, and I can enjoy it. I will give it my full effort; that's all I can do.*

In professional sports and the performing arts, strict discipline is practiced by the greatest and most talented performers in order that their talents and skills might be honed to the highest possible level. They subject themselves to endless hours of demanding practice and exacting standards. They do this to be free of the shackles of mediocrity and to delight in the joy of realized potential. Why should any of us settle for less? Effort devoted to our spiritual development frees us to live life to the fullest. When we see life as an ongoing process—a process that includes challenges as well as easy times—we can accept the fact that some things simply require that we put forth greater effort. That's the way it is. There's nothing wrong, it is just the nature of things.

6

Patience

the stream flows softly
quietly greeting all bends
soon comes a new course
—MICHO

One night we went to see some friends in a production of *Into the Woods* at the Manhattan School of Music. Just as the house lights were dimming and the curtain was about to go up, the man seated to my left shouted at the person in the seat in front of him, "Stop moving around, damn it!" A young man a few seats away shouted back at him, "Hey, that's my father." The first man shouted, "Well, he's a boor!" In an instant, dozens of people were now calling out, "Quiet! Jerk! Shut up!" A riot didn't seem far off, and I found myself agitated and concerned about the potential violence about to break out around me. Fortunately, things settled down as quickly as they had flared up, but it took me quite a few minutes to become completely calm and comfortable again. During the ruckus I felt angry with the man next to me, and the least I wanted to do was give him a really disdainful look so he would know how annoyed I was. (This, while fully aware that he wouldn't care in the least about how annoyed I was.) When I turned in his direction to administer my lethal glance, I noticed for the first time that he was particularly short, and it suddenly occurred to me that perhaps he became upset while trying to find a way to see around the person in front of him. Being a school production, he might have had a relative in the cast and just lost control when he thought he wouldn't be able to see her. My anger melted, and I felt more patient with this fellow's plight. His way of addressing the situation was not particularly gracious, but it is not enough to believe in the virtue of patience, we need to live it with every person we encounter. Fortunately, there always seems to be someone ready to step up and present us with an opportunity to practice patience.

We all have a sense of what patience is, and most of us would acknowledge how easy it can be to lose it. It is as if we think we have a limited supply of this "patience" stuff—perhaps a tiny sack, embedded in each embryo, which expands as we grow, reaching its full capacity of approximately one half-pint when we arrive at physical maturity. Sounds ridiculous, of course, but is it any more foolish than allowing the depletion of that which protects us from the dangers of our own anger, loss of compassion, and reactive behavior? So many of us seem willing to admit that we easily lose our patience and consequently become impatient. Would we so easily admit that we run out of kindness and become unkind, or that we run out of intelligence and become stupid? We have, in fact, an unlimited capacity for patience, far beyond what we might think, and it can be extremely worthwhile to pursue its development. It is the quality of patience that enables us to cope with life's challenges and disruptions with composure and equanimity. If we were saints or Buddhas, we could deal with abuse, insults, lies, and all sorts of adversity with little or no anger, resentment, or desire for retaliation. We would have developed such a depth of lovingkindness and compassion for ourselves and our fellow beings that patience in the face of adversity, insults, and unfair circumstances would seem effortless. Nice, but now let's come back to us not-quite-saints and less-than-Buddha types, we who have to deal with two-year-old Bobby's temper tantrums, traffic jams that resemble parking lots, endless delays at the airport, and being put on terminal hold with Microsoft because we made the mistake of buying the latest version of Windows the day it was released.

Among the qualities we can encourage within ourselves that develop greater patience are acceptance, open-mindedness, compassion, and generosity of spirit. As we strengthen these attributes, we open our hearts and minds and develop more insight into how our thoughts, words, and deeds create happiness or unhappiness for ourselves and others. Patience allows life to feel more spacious and supple. Patience has a transparent quality; it appears effortless. When we are patient, no one senses steam rising from the top of our heads, or clenched fists, gritted teeth, or a mumbled, hell-bent count to ten. There is a naturalness and an ease about us, no matter what the situation. We come to understand that all circumstances and events are impermanent and brought about by innumerable causes and conditions, most of them beyond our control. We give up blaming and instead look for the good in others, even when they seem to be going to great lengths to hide it. Patience is not denial; patience is grace.

The first-century philosopher Epictetus said that one of the signs of moral progress is the gradual extinguishing of blame. Accepting his description, we would have to acknowledge that we've made little moral progress through the ages. Christians blame Jews, Jews blame Muslims, Muslims blame Hindus, Hindus blame Buddhists, and I still blame the city of Los Angeles for seducing the Dodgers away from Brooklyn more than fifty years ago.

The desire to blame someone, or something, for our misfortune arises from anger. When something doesn't go the way we want it to, or the way we think it should, we apparently feel that finding a culprit will somehow rectify the situation, or at least ease our misery. We put considerable effort into finding someone, or something, to blame; we blame the weather, we blame the post office, we blame the doctor, we blame God, but the situation remains what it is. We blame so often and with such intensity that we have become the most litigious society in the history of humankind. We will sue anyone for anything. Certainly, there are times when the best solution may be to turn things over to the courts, but surely we can do so with patience and integrity rather than a burning desire to "get that S.O.B." It is challenging, and sometimes frightening, to accept that things can happen that are totally out of our control. A baby can be born with a serious abnormality; a healthy person can die during minor surgery—accidents happen and no one is at fault. My teenage friends state it most succinctly: "Shit happens," and sometimes there just is no one to blame. More important, blame doesn't change anything. Often the most beneficial path is to accept the reality of the painful, unfortunate situation, spend time with our feelings, and begin to explore our next options.

The venerable teachers, philosophers, and spiritual practitioners throughout history have concluded that the greatest happiness we can experience comes from the development of an open, loving heart. The more we genuinely care about others, the greater our own happiness. For each of us there are those we find easy to get along with and those we find—let's be honest—a royal pain. Those are the people who push our buttons, who appear to be rude, arrogant, or greedy. Ironically, those for whom we feel aversion, whom we would prefer to avoid, are among our most important colleagues if we are to advance spiritually. They become our practice partners. It is with them that we transform theory and philosophy into virtuous action. It is with them that we learn patience. There once was a monk in a monastery who struggled constantly to become more patient. His impatience was a source of misery for himself and those around him. The elders worked with him and tried to teach him about patience but to no avail. The more they tried, and the more he tried, the more impatient he became. So it was decided that he should live alone deep in the forest, where he could meditate solely on the virtues of patience. One day a traveler was journeying through the forest and happened upon the monk's tiny hut. The traveler was surprised to find someone living so far from civilization. He asked the monk why he was living isolated from humanity. The monk told him that he was there to learn patience. The traveler was intrigued and asked how long the monk had been living alone in the forest. The monk replied that he had been there for almost twelve years. The traveler was amazed and also curious. He asked the monk how he would know if he had become patient, since there was no one around with whom he could communicate. The monk growled, "What a stupid question! Go away and leave me to my meditation."

Patience is the direct antithesis of anger. When we are dealing with anger we cannot know happiness, and we are more likely to suffer *disease*, *discomfort*, and *displea*sure. To develop greater patience we need to be aware of the presence of anger as it arises within us. Anger is an emotional state that can vary in intensity from simple annoyance to uncontrollable rage. Thus, it can, in its insidious way, become pervasive if we are not aware of our feelings. When angry, we can become irrational. It can seem as if the entire world is turning against us. We make demands; we want fairness; we want things to be done our way; we want people to agree with us. When we're angry we can become filled with righteous indignation. Why do we, individually and as a nation, go to war as often as we do? Perhaps if we understood that we're experiencing feelings, and feelings are not justification for killing, we might be able to be more patient, step back, and explore peaceful solutions.

Emotions are like seeds that exist within us at a subconscious level. There are seeds of joy, sorrow, happiness, despair, anger, compassion, generosity, and so forth within all of us. As for all seeds, conditions must be right for an emotional seed to flourish, and the mind creates the most important conditions. The mind is the soil in which emotional seeds flourish, lie dormant, or wither. The same event experienced by Jill will be perceived differently by Bill. This is because while we all have the same seeds within us, the soil in which these seeds reside—the mind—is different. One of us isn't right and the other wrong, our experience is simply different. When a seed begins to flourish, we want to encourage the seed of mindfulness to grow along with it. That way, we are aware of anger and other potentially harmful seeds as they sprout and begin to develop. With mindfulness, we remind ourselves that we want to be patient. We must, in fact, be mindful of the destructive power of anger. Buddhism teaches that a moment of anger can destroy lifetimes of virtue. Whether or not we believe in rebirth doesn't matter. Who among us has not experienced in this life the damage, often devastating, of a word spoken in anger? Patience saves relationships; it can even save lives.

I once heard Thich Nhat Hanh say, "Nothing can destroy my peace." My first thought was: *That's fine for him to say. If I had been a monk for sixty years, living primarily in a monastery, as he had, I could make that statement, too.* But then I realized that it is true for me as well; even in the busy secular world in which I live, I can be at peace. So I created a practice for myself of stopping and remembering—remembering that I am the only one who can destroy my peace. Throughout the day, when it seems as if others are making my life difficult, I stop and remind myself that I am the one who determines how I feel about what's going on. I am the one experiencing the words and actions of those around me, and my perceptions are entirely up to me. Realizing that only you can destroy your peace is easy. Remembering not to destroy your peace is *not* always easy. Yet it can be a bit of mischievous fun breathing calmly as others fuss and fume, and thinking to yourself, *You can't destroy my peace. Only I can do that, and I choose not to do so.* You might also silently wish them happiness and good fortune.

 POCKET PRACTICE

Find a place where you can feel completely at ease and say to yourself, *Only I can destroy my peace, and I choose not to do so.*

When performing this practice, locate a place where you will be able to sink deeply into the sensations of peace and calm. A park, a body of water, a garden, and the mountains are excellent choices. Being completely relaxed on a sofa can work well also. Do this practice daily for five minutes for one week, repeating the phrase until you own it. Over time it will become easier to quickly recognize when inner peace is abandoning you, and then you can do the practice again for a few days. When disruption arises around you, you'll have it handy: *Only I can destroy my peace, and I choose not to do so.*

We live in an entirely contingent world—that is, all phenomena arise because of, and in relation to, all other phenomena. This is ongoing in every moment of every day. There are times when we become acutely aware of the contingent nature of our existence. John is already late when he realizes that he forgot his briefcase. It takes him barely a minute to go back, grab the briefcase, and head for the train. But that minute is monumental because as he races for the train, the doors are already closing. He fumes as he waits for the next train. He arrives in the city late and misses his appointment on that fateful morning at the World Trade Center. He spends the rest of his life wondering about miracles, contingencies, God, or simply, "Why?"

My friend Valerie was thrilled when she was accepted into a clinical pastoral education program that would train her toward her goal of becoming a hospital chaplain. They usually require more formal education than Valerie had, but they liked her and sensed the loving nature that would make her a blessing to those in need. Valerie, fatigued by her overbooked schedule, left CPE class one night, hugged a classmate, and stepped into the street too weary to notice the oncoming danger. Perhaps if the class had ended two minutes earlier, or if the hug had lasted a second longer, or if she had stumbled slightly on the sidewalk, then the car that hit her would have passed without incident, and Valerie would be alive. She would live her days never knowing how close she had been to death.

These dramatic events, intricately woven together by the delicate thread of happenstance, call our attention to the contingent nature of all phenomena. But do we live with an awareness that moment to moment, the course of our lives, with every thought, word, and deed, unfolds from the same contingencies and interconnectedness? The Buddha referred to this as "dependent co-arising" or "dependent origination." The circumstances of your existence, and mine, in any given moment are dependent on all the other circumstances in the universe that have preceded this moment. Everything is interconnected through the weaving of cause and effect. When we are aware of the moment-to-moment nature of our existence—including our thoughts, feelings, and sensations—our life experience changes. Energy and effort are balanced with calm and equanimity; wisdom and patience emerge naturally. On those occasions when I've experienced that balanced state, it was clear that I could relax and stop managing the world. I could be patient; everything would unfold as it must.

We are now going to explore a challenging Pocket Practice, one that some readers will question, as have some of my most respected friends and colleagues. However, while there are those who have found this concept difficult to accept, there are many more who have reported that the practice has been eye-opening, and in some cases nothing short of life-altering. Relationships, long a source of torment, have been mended; self-hatred long endured is being relieved. These accounts, often accompanied by tears of gratitude, plus my own positive experience, mean to me that an open mind and a willingness to stretch one's conceptual boundaries can yield meaningful and joyous results. So read on with Beginner's Mind.

Meditation teacher and author Sylvia Boorstein says that when someone asks how she is feeling, she replies that she couldn't be better. She says that it is always true because in that moment, if she could be better, she would be. Let's apply the same straightforward logic to actions. In other words, in each given moment, we are all acting as best we can, because if we could act better, we would. This concept may require some exploration, because when we consider certain words and actions we have experienced, including our own, it can be hard to believe that the person in question was doing their best.

Let's take a look: it is essential to remember that when we say that a person is doing their best, we are referring to a specific action in a specific moment in time. It doesn't mean they couldn't have, or wouldn't have, done better at another time, even seconds earlier or later. It means that specific causes and conditions exist in each unique moment, and contingent on the specifics of each given moment, we act and react as best we can. We are not victims of contingencies, we simply function interconnected with them. As Sylvia Boorstein might say, "If we could have acted better, we would have." That a person *should* have done better may certainly be true, but again, in that moment, with its confluence of causes and conditions, he didn't do what he *should* have done, he did what he did. Is it possible to view his actions, unskillful as they might have been, as the best he could do in that moment?

Our own unskillful behavior presents other complex issues. It can be difficult to accept that when we "lost it" and yelled like a lunatic, or slapped little Jimmy, it was the best we could do in that moment. We often focus, with righteous indignation, on justifying our thoughts, words, and actions or, conversely, feeling bad about them. We insist that that was not the best we could have done and bypass the reality that if we could have done better, we would have. Our egos don't like the part of us that behaved poorly. We confuse "I should have acted better" with the reality of the moment—we didn't. Yet again, can we accept that in that moment, that was the best we could do? It can be quite challenging.

Now, what about the person whose actions are repeatedly abusive, mean, or violent? Can we see that even that person, as nasty and perhaps as dangerous as their actions may be, is still doing the best they can in each specific moment? Repeated abusive behavior may mean that a particular person does not function on a level we find acceptable or that we want to be near. That person's best may simply be unacceptable or even unsafe. This can be particularly difficult if the person is a relative, or if we have become involved in an intimate relationship with such a person, or if the individual has authority over us in the workplace. The fact that this person is doing his best doesn't mean that it is necessarily good enough for our circumstance. We're not practicing how to become a doormat. We're striving for greater meaning and joy in our lives. That can mean taking action to stop an abusive or violent situation. Sometimes it is deemed necessary to remove someone from society for the safety and well-being of all concerned, but by understanding that even that person is doing the best he can, we can take firm action in a compassionate way rather than being vindictive or malicious. "Everyone is doing their best" is not a judgment, as in *good, better, best,* nor should it be used to support a derogatory view, such as, "Oh, the poor jerk is doing the best he can." It is also not a cop-out for our own lack of effort, as in, "What do you want? I'm doing my best."

It may be uncomfortable to accept, but when you were ending that relationship a few years ago and spoke so harshly to your ex, you were doing the best you could. Today, of course, you might be more gracious. The business partner who stole from you might have been overwhelmed with fear or greed. Although his actions were terrible at the time, as conditions came together, it was the best he could do. It's hard to believe, isn't it? Make no mistake though, if his actions were illegal, retribution may be morally and legally appropriate. If his repeated actions are abusive, unkind, or offensive, it may be time to end the relationship. One's best doesn't necessarily mean that it is good enough. It is simply the way things are that one's best is often not good enough. The young girl who wants more than anything to be a professional ballerina or the boy who wants to play for the Yankees may have to learn this. Some dreams will remain dreams, and some hopes will never be realized. One key to happiness is to still enjoy dancing and playing baseball. Another key is to not accept abuse or unkind behavior.

Can we see beyond the details to the larger picture? It requires patience, compassion, and an open heart and mind. One of the major obstacles to this type of clear vision is what I call "the judgmental mind." When someone acts in a way that is abusive, or even illegal, it can seem impossible that the person was doing his or her best. We see only the unacceptable deed and lose sight of the complete picture. On reflection, we can come to understand that the awful decision was all that person could see in that moment. An action can be terribly unskillful and, at the same time, still be the best a person can come up with. When we get caught up in continually judging the action, our own or another's, we can lose sight of all else. The action, though unacceptable, was the best the person could do. Now you decide how to respond.

When we proceed patiently, we become more accepting of ourselves and others; life flows more easily, and we become a friend to the beings on this planet. Understanding that we, and those around us, are doing our best helps us see with greater clarity, speak and act with more patience, and experience less annoyance and grief. Understanding that we are all doing our best is not only a legitimate view, it is a kinder, more compassionate way of living. As we gradually accept that we and all beings are doing our best, constriction releases and a spaciousness opens within us. Acceptance allows room for spiritual growth, and we notice that in many instances we now do better than what was previously our best.

Remember the man who was sitting next to me in the theater and suddenly "lost it"? When I saw how difficult it was for him to see past the person in front of him, I immediately realized that he was doing the best he could. It was an instantaneous response rather than a process of rationalization. His actions weren't gracious, kind, or skillful, but in that moment it was the best he could do. Besides, even if it wasn't, thinking that it was changed my experience from fear, anger, and discomfort to compassion, kindheartedness, and ease. And perhaps, after all, that's the real point. Debating whether one's father should have done better, or whether Hitler could possibly have been doing his best, or whether there is such a thing as pure evil in this world will do little to bring greater happiness to your life. Viewing the actions of all beings as the best they could do in that moment can lighten *this* moment for you. For now, maybe that's enough.

Understand and accept that in each given moment,
everyone, including you, is doing the best they can.

When I officiate a wedding ceremony, I often say to
the bride and groom, "At this joyous moment, it might
seem impossible that either of you could ever be angry
with the other. But you are both adults and know something about human nature. Please remember always, in
moments of disagreement, the person with whom you
are disagreeing, the person with whom you are angry,
is also the person you love." All of life is about relationships, beginning with our relationship with ourself.
Patience nurtures the joy in relationships and diminishes
its difficulties. Think to yourself often, *I'm doing my best.
He's doing his best.*

There is a legend that tells of a king who challenged
his wise men to create a phrase that would always be
true no matter what the time, place, or conditions. They
thought, they contemplated, and they meditated for many
weeks before they finally presented the king with a tablet

inscribed with the words "This too shall pass." Ever since then these words have humbled the prideful and offered hope to the afflicted.

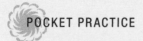

POCKET PRACTICE

Write these words on a dozen little pieces of paper and strategically place them where you'll see them often: "Patience. This too shall pass."

7

Truthfulness

in the stillness of
a soft moonlit field beyond
the wind whispers true
—MICHO

I n 2008, a remarkable event that drew national attention happened at a college softball game in Ellensburg,
Washington. It is a story about a few young women
finding greater truth within themselves than perhaps
they knew existed. It is also about what truly matters.

Sara, a smallish senior on the Western Oregon team,
hit what looked like a three-run home run against Central Washington. Never in her twenty-one years had she
hit a ball over the fence, so it was understandable that as
she ran toward first base she got caught up in watching
the flight of the ball. Awestruck by what she was seeing,

she missed touching first base. Alerted by the screams of her teammates, she turned quickly back to step on the base, but as she did she twisted her right knee, sending her toppling to the ground as she touched the base. Her coach made sure no teammates touched Sara, because the rules stated that if they did, she would not have been allowed to continue around the bases. The umpires huddled and ruled that if Sara could not make it around the bases, two runs would score but she would be credited with only a single. Then the big first baseman for Central Washington approached the umpires with a stunning suggestion. She asked if it would it be okay if she and her teammates carried Sara around the bases so she could touch each one. The umpires consulted and said it would be legal. So two strong Central Washington players lifted Sara and carried her to second base, and gently lowered her so she could touch the base. Then, through tears and laughter, the three of them continued their extraordinary procession to third base, and then home plate. Everyone in attendance stood and cheered, many with tears in their eyes, for they knew they were witnessing something special, something they would remember for a very long time.

As she was taken to the hospital for surgery to repair a torn ligament, Sara's college softball career came to an end with an unimpressive .153 batting average, and just one home run—one extraordinary home run.

It has been said that great baseball players don't make great managers. To the exceptionally talented player so much just comes naturally, and he usually functions best by going out and allowing his gifts to flow freely. The lesser player has to be constantly working, studying, and practicing just to retain a spot on the team. He has to learn the game inside and out, physically, mentally, and emotionally, to enhance whatever natural talent he may have. Still, this often results in only a brief playing career of little note. However, the effort put forth can lead to greater insights into the finer points of the game, and that creates the potential for a first-rate manager.

I was raised in an environment where truth was not valued. Falsifying, exaggeration, and aggrandizement were the norm, and thus what I learned. Throughout my childhood I would hear my father saying things that simply weren't true. I hardly noticed after a while because so often they were stories about the most inane things, like that we went to the beach yesterday, which we had not, or that he had landed a certain job, which he had not. Self-aggrandizement was a practice witnessed and well learned by the male members of our family, and I was no exception. With this background, I started out, in a manner of speaking, without much talent or insight when it came to truthfulness. I was a minor-leaguer with a lot of learning, and unlearning, to do if I was ever to breathe the rarified air of the major leagues of dignity, virtue, and honor. Uprooting pretense so that truthfulness can emerge is serious business requiring mindfulness and determination. I have had to practice truthfulness diligently, and it has not always been easy—habit energy, fear, and ignorance are powerful forces. Consequently, I've always needed to be mindful of my speech, mindful because I could at any time fall back into what I had learned in my earliest years—that which for me is no longer acceptable. In that light, I feel well equipped to address the subject of truthfulness.

Jesus said, "The truth will set you free." My own experience has been that while the truth may set you free, it can come at a hefty price. For the truth to set us free, we must be willing to shed the layers of subtle, protective self-deception we have created so as not to face our fears, insecurities, and doubts. Breaking free in this way—letting go of our falseness and embracing our true self—is one of the most challenging and gratifying of human experiences. We learn that we are each truly amazing creatures. As one Zen master put it, "We are all perfect, and we need a little work."

Dr House, the title character in a popular television series, declares repeatedly that accessing an accurate diagnosis is impossible because everyone lies. Therefore, he can never get accurate information from patients. Invariably, it turns out that he is right, his patients have been lying. Of course, it also turns out that House (the pot) lies more than any of the kettles. Several years ago, the cover story of a major weekly news magazine declared in a bold headline, "Everyone Lies." As I read through the troubling article, I began to wonder if the final line was going to be "None of this is true; we're lying." (It wasn't.)

The heart-wrenching tragedy of Shakespeare's *Othello* illustrates the destructive force of jealousy, but Othello's green-eyed downfall is born of Iago's insidious deception. Iago knows that even the fearless Othello has his insecurities, and with masterful cunning manipulates the hero. Othello, blinded by suspicion, can no longer see the truth and destroys his love and his life. This is extraordinary theater, but how many of us in real life have been wounded at one time or another by the venom of a false tongue? Likewise, have we experienced the discomfort of remorse in the wake of a misleading statement of our own?

On a lighter note, a man named Jamal goes to the house of his friend Eli. "My friend," says Jamal, "I have a great deal of heavy work to do today. May I borrow your ox to help me?" Eli replies, "Ah, my friend, I would gladly lend you my ox, but she is not here. I have loaned her to another for a few days. So sorry." Jamal leaves and is only a few steps outside the door when he hears the distinct bellow of Eli's ox coming from behind the house. Jamal confronts Eli, saying, "My friend, you told me that you loaned the ox to someone else, but I just heard the animal's voice from behind your house." Eli responds, "My friend, are you going to believe me or that stupid beast?"

There is probably nothing we could do that would have a more immediate positive effect on our lives and on those around us than becoming more mindful of the words we speak. We are constantly communicating, and our words have enormous power—the power to inspire, encourage, comfort, and uplift. Unfortunately, they can also cut, wound, and cause profound, long-lasting sorrow. There is considerable emphasis in the Buddhist teachings on skillful speech. Skillful speech is defined as speaking truthfully, compassionately, usefully, and supportively. If we are to speak skillfully, in a way that alleviates sorrow and anxiety for ourselves and others, we must speak truthfully. We won't even tell little white lies, nor will we exaggerate, minimize, or self-aggrandize. These forms of unskillful speech often come from a fear that what we are is not good enough, which is simply not true. We may not be the right person for a specific job, or a particular relationship, but that does not diminish our value as human beings. If we find that from time to time we bend the truth in order to get what we believe we want, we might need to evaluate what is most important to us. When we look deeply, we find that there is always a better way to achieve something significant than lying or deceiving. In addition, a simple practice would be to follow T-shirt wisdom: "Tell the truth. There'll be less to remember."

So, where, when, and how do the seeds of truthfulness get planted? The phone rings and we say to our five-year-old, "Jimmy, please answer the phone, and if it's Jane, tell her I'm not here." That sounds innocent enough, but what is the underlying message we are conveying to our children? Are we teaching that a little lie is okay because what we are doing right now is more important than being truthful? Besides, what's the big deal about a little fib? Well, it may not seem like a big deal, but we know that every giant oak began as a tiny seed, and the

Grand Canyon was once a small crack in the ground. An alternative worth considering that would take only a moment longer would be to show by example what it is to be truthful. We could take the phone and say to Jane, "Hi, I'm swamped right now. Can I call you back?" By doing so we show that we honor our friends and trust that they will understand. Further, we *do* call them back, because we said we would. We are all role models and teachers. Good teachers are wise, compassionate, humble, and truthful. There is a Zen teaching which says that when you study with a master, listen carefully to his words and, perhaps more important, watch how he peels his orange and puts on his sandals. We need to be aware that children notice everything. Our actions, too, must be truthful.

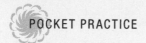 POCKET PRACTICE

Think before speaking, particularly in the presence of children.

We always want to be mindful of our words but especially if feeling annoyed or impatient—states that even the most angelic of children can occasionally bring about. Little eyes and ears take in everything. With every thought, word, and deed you are influencing the life of a young person. You are affecting your life as well, but we'll come to that.

It was parents' day at school, and my six-year-old, Samantha, was terribly excited because we were going to meet her new best friend, Alicia. When we arrived at school we were ushered into the cafeteria, where a brood of energetic progeny were dragging their delighted (I think) parents from the art room to science projects to friends to teachers. Samantha came running over and immediately pointed into a throng of adorable munchkins and yelled over the din, "That's Alicia; that's my best friend." "Which one, sweetie?" I asked. "That one, the one in the white shirt, that's Alicia." There were so many wearing white shirts that I couldn't possibly have known which was Alicia, clearly annoying Sam to no end. "The tall one," she said firmly, which narrowed it down to about four or five. After more pointing and frustration, she finally demanded, "You wait here!" Upon which she ran over and grabbed a tall, adorable munchkin in a white shirt and dragged her over to us. "This is Alicia. This is my best friend."

That was more than twenty-five years ago, and what remains vivid in my memory is that although Alicia was the only African-American child in the room at that time, it never occurred to Sam to use her skin color as a way to identify her. Surely it would have been easier, and who could have faulted her? However, Sam, an innocent six-year-old, was color-blind, and in that moment I realized that I was not. It doesn't mean that I am a bigot or a racist, which I hope and believe I am not, but the inner search for truth must be an ongoing process, because we are constantly changing. Statements that begin, "I am the kind of person who . . ." or "I would never . . ." suggest a belief that we are some sort of solid, fixed configuration, and that simply is not so. We exhibit traits and characteristics, and we have a history that may make our response to a given situation somewhat predictable, but the law of impermanence always applies—everything changes.

Truthfulness begins at home, so to be truthful begins with being honest with one's self. We need to see ourselves as we really are, not as we would like to believe we are.

The Swiss psychologist Carl Jung advised us to always be aware of what he called our "shadow side," that which can be dark and irrational, the side we can so easily deny.

The shadow is a real part of ourselves, a part that we may not find appealing. We all have a shadow side, and the less it is acknowledged and examined, the more dense and impenetrable it can become. When we are aware of our weaknesses or negative tendencies, we open the opportunity to work on them. But if they are repressed or denied, they never get addressed. That very denial, said Jung, can be dangerous. Furthermore, accepting the truth about who we really are is the only way we can be aware of our true feelings and alert to the words and deeds those feelings can motivate. Truthfulness begins with being who we are, not some image we may have of ourselves, and not trying to present someone we think others want us to be. Further, we are not who we used to be, and we are not yet who we might become. It helps to remember that we don't have to believe everything we think, including our thoughts about ourselves.

The most important step in developing skillful, truthful speech is to become more mindful of our thoughts and feelings before speaking. As we develop greater mindfulness we can more easily sense when it would be wise to stop, breathe, and consider what we are about to say before saying it. But speaker beware, life comes at us quickly. A casual conversation can turn ever so subtly and imperceptibly and become contentious and confrontational. Pointed comments can insidiously slip from our mouths and damage a previously cherished relationship. We need to be aware of subtle changes in our feelings and emotions while conversing, because they will influence the way we speak. These concepts are by no means unique to Buddhism. Jesus taught that it isn't what we put into our mouths that defiles us but rather what comes out.

While we can apologize for something we said, we can never really take back our words. In the time of the Buddha there was no law against slander, but he advised against it and its nasty little brother, gossip, because he saw the suffering that this kind of unskillful speech can cause. There is an old Hasidic tale of a villager who was feeling deep remorse for the harm his gossip had caused his neighbor. He went to his rabbi to seek advice. The rabbi suggested that he go to the market and buy a chicken, pluck it completely, and bring it to him. When the man returned with the featherless bird, the rabbi told him to now retrace his steps and gather every one of the scattered feathers. The man replied that it would be impossible to do so because by now the feathers were likely blown throughout the many neighboring villages. The rabbi nodded in agreement, and the man understood. He saw that it is not possible to take back our words.

In the seventeenth century, the Zen poet Basho wrote this Haiku gem:

The temple bell stops
but the sound keeps coming
out of the flowers.

One of the greatest causes of conflict in relationships is when people feel they are not being heard. Because the brain is so capable, we often assume we know what the other person is going to say before they say it, and we jump in and respond before they finish. I had a counseling client who complained that her husband never listened to her, and when he did, he always told her she was wrong. "He's such a jerk," she told me. I suggested that name-calling might not be the most effective way to remedy the situation, but that perhaps the next time they had a discussion, she pause for five seconds before speaking and in that time try to get in touch with her feelings, then begin her next sentence with: "I feel . . ."

When she returned for her next session I asked how things were going and she said, "Terrible. I tried your suggestion and it didn't work. I took my time, got in touch with my feelings, and said, 'I feel you're the biggest asshole I ever met.'"

All of the exercises suggested here work best
when carried out with at least a smidgen of wisdom.

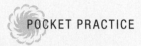

POCKET PRACTICE

Develop listening skills.

This practice can dramatically change relationships. The first step to becoming a good listener is to remind yourself that you care about the person who is speaking. The next step in developing listening skills is to let go of your thoughts while the other person is speaking. Notice if, as the other speaks, your mind is already preparing a response. You may be agreeing or disagreeing, or perhaps thinking of advice to offer. If so, gently release your thoughts and return to listening. Determine that you will not respond until you have left at least a five-second period of silence. This may seem long and awkward at first, but stay with it. The rewards can be great. A variation is to quietly take three complete breaths before responding. The other person doesn't know you're doing this, but they do know they're not being interrupted, and that will feel good. They may also have the sense that you are considering what they have said—which, by the way, is not a bad practice, either.

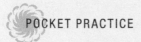

POCKET PRACTICE

You need only a one-word practice when it comes to teasing: *don't!*

Although teasing entails a creative use of words, it is always at someone's expense, and it often hurts more than folks let on. No one wants to appear to be overly sensitive or to not have a sense of humor. You could use your same wondrous mind that created a tease to fashion a truthful, kind, and uplifting remark instead. That would be creative skillful speech, and a beautiful practice to tuck into any pocket. People would benefit more from your presence and want to be around you. You would bring more positive energy to your relationships.

Here is an exercise that I find incredibly enlightening. To be truthful, I didn't create this, and I'm not sure who originally did, but I'm certain they would be happy to have us all practice it. It is about freeing one's self from the tendency to gossip. Gossip is defined as speaking about someone who is not physically present. Strictly speaking, it has nothing to do with whether what we say is positive or negative. If the person about whom we are speaking is not present, it is gossip, and gossip is considered one of the most destructive forms of unskillful speech.

 POCKET PRACTICE

Do not speak about anyone who is not physically present.

Do this practice for a specified period of time—let's say seven days. That's the whole practice, short and sweet—do not speak about anyone who is not right there with you. It may sound easy, but the first time I did it I was shocked. Now I do the exercise two or three times a year, for a week or two at a time. My voice gets a good rest, as I find myself participating in many fewer conversations. I also find that there is a residual effect after each week of practice. I'm more aware of my speech, especially if I begin to speak about someone who is not present. To be sure, there are instances when it is necessary to speak about someone who is not there. A doctor might have to discuss a patient's condition with his family, or a business decision might need to be made involving someone who is not present at the meeting. In those situations, keep references to the nonattending party as brief as possible and speak as if that person were there. It is enough to say, "I think Jane is the best choice to work with this client," without adding, "and besides, John is an idiot."

Today, when we consider skillful speech, we must look at a phenomenon that did not exist in the time of the Buddha: e-mail. Every day millions of e-mail messages are sent and received, and the potential for the unskillful use of words is enormous. Consider first that with the advent of the telephone, we became a people that for the most part abandoned the practice of letter writing. Then came the computer and the age of electronic mail. Like everything else associated with computers, e-mail moves at lightning-fast speed and can easily lure us onto the fast track of rapid communication. What a perfect recipe for the unskillful use of words—a people unpracticed at letter writing and the capability to churn out one quick letter after another.

POCKET PRACTICE

Before clicking the send button on the e-mails you write, stop, close your eyes, and breathe for a few seconds.

It is an excellent practice to reread each e-mail before sending it and make sure it contains nothing you might later regret having said. Let thoughts like *What is my intention?* and *Am I being considerate?* go through your mind. If the e-mail can be changed to better reflect the person you want to be, make the changes. The whole process doesn't have to take a long time. Besides, it is unlikely that you would have something more important to do. Even your e-mails should reflect your true self.

POCKET PRACTICE

When you feel that a conversation is about to become heated, stop and consider what you are about to say before saying it.

We can usually sense when a conversation is about to become strained. That's the time to stop for a moment, before things turn contentious. You can avoid tremendous grief if you remember that you can never really take back your words. Find a way to express your truth with kindness.

We are all such perfect beings just as we are. It is when we lose contact with our perfection—our true self—that we feel the need to appear other than what we really are.

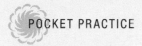

POCKET PRACTICE

Before going to bed at night, write down one truth you learned that day.

Most of us become more focused and specific when we write. You will never have this day again; bring to mind something you learned.

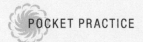

POCKET PRACTICE

One day each month, every time you are about to speak, stop for a moment and consider if what you are about to say will improve upon the silence.

It is said that silence is golden. It can be challenging to improve upon golden silence, but with just one day a month of concentrated awareness, we can make our words glitter with kindness, grace, and dignity.

8

Determination

darting through rapids
fish jump hawks soar swans afloat
the stream laughs loudly
—MICHO

As I was driving on that icy, cold Saturday night in January, a heavy thudlike fatigue suddenly hit me. It was as if someone had flicked a switch and the lights went out. Then, after a few seconds, just as suddenly, the switch was flicked on and I was fully awake again. Nevertheless, I pulled over at the next opportunity and stopped for gas, and with a healthy dose of cold, fresh air in my lungs, I felt refreshed and ready to continue driving. It had been less than twenty-four hours since Susanna and I had returned from three weeks of business and pleasure in India. We had driven to New

Jersey to share in the joy of a dear friend's wedding. Now, heading home and approaching our highway exit, I asked Susanna if she would like me to drop her off at home or if she would like to come with me to the garage. That's the last thing I remember except for a fleeting awareness that we were in immediate grave danger. A thought wafted gently through my mind: *I am about to die.* Then there was a feeling of floating upward, out of the body, leaving everything behind, perhaps dying. I have no memory of the crash.

The next thing I remember was seeing a smoking air bag inches from my face. I was covered with blood, and there was glass everywhere. I asked Susanna if she was all right. "Yes. Are you?" she answered. "Yes," I replied, aware that I was conscious but not much else. We were driving a high-end SUV, and it was crumpled like paper all around us. It was pitch-black, and all we could see was that there was traffic moving on the road above us. I wasn't able to move very much with the steering wheel pressed close to my chest, nor could we open the doors or windows. I thought to turn off the engine, but it was already off. I tried to turn it on, hoping we could open a window, but everything was dead, except, it seemed, for Susanna and me.

Susanna saw that the back window was completely

blown out, and she felt she could crawl back there and climb through the opening. With the gracefulness that told of her years as a dancer, she slid through the broken glass and jagged metal and out the back window. Considering my awkward position behind the steering wheel, and how covered I was with blood, it seemed best for me to just wait patiently and contain my desire to extricate myself from the tangle of steel and debris. My male ego was put on hold as my brave wife crawled out of the wreckage to seek help.

Within minutes firemen were trying to pull open a door to get me out, but none would yield, even to those big, determined heroes. They brought down some equipment and pried a door open. Now the police and emergency medical team were on the scene, and I was gently removed from the smoldering rubble, had a restraining collar placed on me, and was strapped to a board. I kept insisting that they attend to Susanna as well, because, after all, she had been in the same accident. "We're taking care of her, but your injuries are more serious," I was told. This assessment was apparently made because I was so covered with blood. However, they did then strap Susanna to a gurney, and side by side in an ambulance we were carted off to Roosevelt Hospital.

The police told us that our vehicle apparently went

down an embankment, rolled over, and crashed into a wall and a tree. It was completely destroyed, and it seemed miraculous that anyone could have survived such a crash. When I saw the vehicle a few days later, it was indeed a shocking sight. I don't know why we didn't die that night, but being involved with many spiritually minded people, we were offered various philosophies and spiritual views. I particularly liked the one from our pragmatic auto dealer: "God, in the form of seat belts and air bags, can work miracles." Susanna was jolted and had some muscular aches and pains, and I had a number of minor cuts and a jammed finger. I think that much of the blood the rescue workers saw on me must have been from cuts sustained when the air bags deployed. By five in the morning we were home from the hospital and decided that we would lead the Community Sunday session scheduled to begin in a few hours, but we would not discuss our mishap with anyone until afterward. Later, when folks learned what had happened, many seemed amazed that we had come to lead the service. Yet for us it was pretty straightforward. We were a bit shaken but felt perfectly capable of carrying on, and while I had never thought of it quite this way, with our long history as professional performers, there probably is a lot of determined "show must go on" stuff in our veins. (Truthfully, in all my years in the theater, I never really understood why the show had to go on. "The power must be restored," "the food must be delivered," and "the ambulance must get through" all seem more significant, but why does a show have to go on? I don't know. Perhaps it is the drama of the theater.)

The eruption of feelings and emotions that follows a near-death experience, or any event that causes us to stop and look deeply at the reality of our lives, is ripe with the potential for insight and clarity. Often we can sense, at such times, the possibility of a deep and powerful awakening— and with it, a clearer sense that our time in this life is not unlimited. This can lead to a period of inspired determination to address areas of our life that could benefit from change. A few years ago I worked with a young client who was diagnosed with breast cancer. Only a few months earlier, her mother had died of the same disease. I was impressed and moved by the resolve, strength of character, and spirit of this twenty-four-year-old warrior. One day she told me that while she looked forward to getting back to her career, when she was finished with this illness she would not go back to living life as she had before. If she did, then the illness, and all she was going through, would be for nothing.

Spiritual practice, in whatever form, is not easy. We

are challenged by a complex world around us, and an even more complex world within us. Twenty-five hundred years ago in northern India, Siddhartha Gautama, a young man of means, left a life of luxury to explore life's deepest truths. After years of study with the renowned teachers of his time, and after subjecting himself to extreme austerities, he felt he was close to enlightenment. Finally, he sat down beneath a ficus tree (later to be known as the bodhi tree) and vowed not to get up until he had reached a state of complete enlightenment. The legend tells of how Gautama was assailed again and again through the long night by Mara, the demon, the destroyer of virtuous pursuits. Throughout the night, a determined, resolute Gautama resisted the attacks and temptations brought by Mara; overcame his powerful, destructive presence; and became a fully awakened being—a Buddha. It is important to realize that Gautama was a human being just like us. He was not a god or any kind of divine being. Through clear intention, courage, and determination, he achieved his goal.

Mara exists within us all and manifests as our doubts, fears, greed, hatred, and ignorance. He is temptation, distraction, and falseness, and he fashions our unskillful thoughts, words, and actions. He makes the negative seem appealing and the positive seem without worth.

He is death in the form of the destroyer of spiritual life. The most saintly among us are visited by Mara; no one is exempt. Just like Gautama, we can focus on our aspiration and overcome Mara with determination, grit, and guts. When we become determined, things begin to move in the direction we want. As we experience even small successes, we feel a sense of joyous courage strengthening within us.

Determination in the Buddhist context is about the perseverance to stay with the dharma—the teachings of the Buddha—even when we are assailed by doubts and misgivings. No matter what tradition we follow, if any, when we commit to living a more spiritual, more meaningful, life, there will be times when we will need the full extent of our determination and fortitude. It is this determination that will help us stay the course, overcome doubt, resist temptation, and face our demons. Such determination is often accompanied by a deep sense of joy, because although the road may be bumpy at times, we know we are moving toward truth, wholeness, and freedom. This newfound resolve becomes inspired by glimmers of insight into our true self—our loving, generous, compassionate self. Perseverance and satisfaction grow as we overcome obstacles that might otherwise have stopped us. Determination strengthens determination.

My father had a two-by-four that was reserved for "disciplining" my brother and me. This disciplining was called a "spanking," but its frequency and level of intensity could have earned it another label. However, as any woman who has given birth can attest, physical pain is temporal and usually fades into the far reaches of memories lost. As a child, I had no knowledge of my father's mental illness. As a young adult, my experience of his abusiveness, violence, and threatening behavior was that they erupted so quickly and ferociously that they needed to be addressed without delay. There was no time to consider my feelings; immediate action was necessary, often crucial. More than once I accompanied the police as they carted my resistant dad to a psychiatric hospital. I believe my emotions and feelings related to my father were deeply buried by a protective psyche, but, as I was to learn, to be buried is not necessarily to be extinguished.

A few years after my father died, a friend's father also passed away. I visited him as he observed the Jewish tradition of *shivah*, a seven-day period of mourning. In the presence of his grief and sorrow, I felt envious for the sadness he was feeling. He loved his father and would miss him. When my father died, I experienced no loss or grief, and now, years later, I felt the emptiness of that absence of feeling. Well, perhaps "absence of feeling" is not entirely correct. Relationships don't necessarily end because one party is no longer physically present, and the emotional part of my relationship with my father was, at that point, one of discomfort and confusion. I felt I could do better, and I decided that exploring that relationship would be worth the effort. Therapy and meditation, already significant in my life, took on a new focus, and the journey was not easy. I saw that I had suppressed for decades an array of conflicting feelings, including anger, resentment, and fear. There were times when the work was wrenching and debilitating, but I was determined and often buoyed by a glimmer of light that seemed to confirm that this was the right action for me. I knew I could be a kinder, more compassionate person, and I sensed that for that to happen, this "root relationship" had to be healed. There had to be a way to truly forgive and free myself from the fetters of negativity. Slowly I made progress, and as I broke through there emerged not only forgiveness but a genuine sense of gratitude for my father, and for the challenging childhood I had lived. The breakthrough penetrated my entire being. It was enormous and gratifying, but the work still seemed incomplete.

A few years later, on Father's Day, I stood before the Community of Peace and Spirituality and spoke about my father with tears in my eyes. In fact, there were tears in most everyone's eyes that morning as I shared the next step, the ultimate breakthrough I had made in my relationship with my dad. I told how it was now more than twenty years since he had passed away and how aspects of our relationship continued to evolve, how through determination and perseverance I had come to a place of forgiveness and understanding, and how out of that understanding came a deep sense of gratitude. I felt thankful to my father for providing me with life and invaluable life experiences. Yet with all of that, what was painfully missing was that I had never figured out how to love him. Then, in preparing my talk for that Father's Day morning, it just happened. The difficult past had softened and allowed room for memories, memories long buried—memories of holding his hand as a boy of seven or eight as we walked up the ramp into Ebbets Field to see a Dodgers game (which he sat through even though it was of no particular interest to him). I remembered how he loved my head resting on his lap when I was tired—a rare but special moment for him—how he was the one I ran to when I saw my friend get hit by a car, or the time I accidentally hit a friend while swinging a baseball bat.

In many ways, when I needed him, he was there. I don't know how capable he was of being present, but he was there. How could I not love him for that?

I envisioned him as a boy of fifteen, pulled out of school to manage the growing family business, devastated because all he wanted was to be a doctor. He never spoke about it, but every book in our house was about some aspect of medical practice. He was not able to deal with my mother's death; she was forty-four and he was forty-seven, and his bipolar condition worsened. He did fairly well while on medication but could be harmful to himself and others when he decided he didn't need it. One day I went to visit him, and as I drove up to his house I saw him holding a young woman on the ground and wielding an ax over her head. I was able to grab him and pull him off her. He was arrested and spent the final ten days of his life in a forensic ward. I visited him only once, and he was alone when he died. Later, I regretted that. I wish I had been wise enough to have wanted to hold his hand as he died.

It took time, but with gentle yet firm determination, I came to love the man whose final words to me were, "You're no damn good. You never were, and you never will be." I knew he was ill and off his medication. I knew he was not a perfect father, but neither am I. Mostly I had come to understand that he had done the best he could. I could have quit on my father—it would have been a lot easier—but I'm so grateful that I stayed the course. I appreciate myself for having the courage, and I appreciate what my friend Wayne Muller refers to as the spiritual advantages of a painful childhood. I am, today, deeply grateful for those advantages.

In dealing with the negativity resulting from extended anger, old hurts, wounds, and injustices, it can help to ask yourself, *What would I have to give up to be free from this anger, this turmoil, and these negative feelings I've been holding on to for so long?* That might seem like an odd concept at first—*what would I have to give up?* After all, when we are abused, beaten, or raped, so much is taken from us. Why would we now explore giving up more? The reality is that in this world there are those who do thoughtless, heinous, and illegal things. Even with the best intentions, any of us can harm another. Young, inexperienced people have children, and although they do their best, their parenting can be unskillful and leave scars. Accidents, illnesses, hurricanes, tsunamis, fires, and earthquakes occur and leave terrible suffering in their wake. When we are victimized we can become angry—angry with a parent, an attacker, our body, or our God. An injury or illness may leave us physically or emotionally challenged for the remainder of our lives, often requiring considerable adjustments to the way we function in our daily activities. Long after our physical pain subsides, our suffering continues. Yet at a certain point, each of us can make a transformative decision. Although victimized, we can begin the process of healing—of no longer thinking of ourselves as victims. This can be the most challenging work we will ever do, but determination and an optimistic appreciation of our own efforts can get us through to a happier and more meaningful life.

To advance spiritually requires a method of practice and the determination to carry it out. Slowly our practice intermingles with our daily activities and permeates our actions until all of life becomes our spiritual practice. Many of us read books, practice yoga, and attend workshops, seminars, and religious services, and yet we're still burdened by deep fears and anxiety. With our objective clearly in mind, we can look directly at our demons, do battle with them, and emerge triumphantly. Franklin Delano Roosevelt, a man who faced physical challenges and enormous responsibilities, said, "The only thing we have to fear is fear itself." Well, sometimes we feel afraid and we don't even know why we're afraid. We wake up in the morning feeling fearful, or out of nowhere, fear and anxiety just seem to appear. It can help to remember that even though it can manifest in various parts of the body, the only place fear can exist is in the mind. It is part of spiritual practice to do battle with our fears. We may think sometimes that we're not making progress, but as long as we continue to practice with skillful awareness and determination, we are advancing. Even as we struggle, we're awakening, stimulating, and advancing our highest self—our true self.

Have great reverence for yourself. The spiritual journey is traveled on a glorious highway, but it also goes through dingy neighborhoods like confusion, doubt, and insecurity. Nevertheless, it can be a joyous ride. As we allow our positive energy to be present and to strengthen, we encourage and stimulate our true loving nature, our compassion, and our generous spirit. We can work hard with courage and determination, and at the same time enjoy the ride, smile at our mistakes, and get back up and begin again, and again, and again. That's the joy of determination.

Determination is a mental strength we call on, over and over again—often over a long period of time—that is focused on a specific goal or goals. So, while determination is usually a long-term practice, like everything else in life, it can be practiced only in the present moment. Thinking ahead about how determined you will be to resist when the dessert tray is offered at dinner tonight is not as effective as determination employed at the very moment of temptation. I used to teach my students a practice to use each January when they were writing their first checks or letters of the year. Habit energy pulls us to write the date of the year that just ended rather than the new year. Thinking about it in the morning, when you will not be writing checks until that evening, is not very effective. If, however, we stop when we write the J of January and say, "Ah, it's now 2010," we have an effective practice.

Determination is necessary for all of our other practices to be effective. It is determination that provides the energy for change. Even if you commit just a few minutes a day, practice with both enthusiasm and patience. This is *your* journey; it is not about anyone else, and it cannot be compared to another. Don't yield; keep the faith.

 POCKET PRACTICE

Remind yourself often that you are mentally strong—
you can do it.

Determination is a mental quality, so just as we can train the body, we can train the mind. When life is challenging, tell yourself often that you are equal to the challenge—you can do it. Remind yourself that hanging in just a bit longer can make all the difference. Repeat one or more of these phrases often throughout the day: "I don't quit!" "I am strong!" "Yes, I can!" To paraphrase Gandhi: be the change you want to see in the world.

 POCKET PRACTICE

Don't hold grudges—find a way to forgive.

Look to the great teachers for inspiration. Jesus of Nazareth suffered excruciating pain and chose to forgive his tormenters. The Dalai Lama and the Zen monk Thich Nhat Hanh see all people as their friends, even those who have treated them poorly. Follow their example. Find a way to let the other person off the hook, even if you think they don't deserve it. Do it for you. If you are determined to keep an open heart and be a loving presence in the world, you will be able to do it. You may even find that it gets easier with practice.

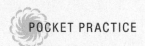

POCKET PRACTICE

For five minutes, focus on a specific object, bringing the mind back to the object each time it wanders.

This is a short exercise, based on the practice of insight meditation, that can be used to gently develop determination. Sit quietly, relaxed, comfortable, and at the same time alert, with the back straight. Select an object on which to focus your concentration for a few minutes. It might be the breath, the sounds in the room, the sensations in the body, or anything that you can comfortably focus on for five minutes. You can do this with your eyes open or closed, whichever is more comfortable. As the mind wanders, and it will, gently return your awareness to the object of concentration, again and again. Use light-hearted determination, not judgments or self-criticism. You cannot do anything wrong. The mind may appear to have a mind of its own. Allow yourself to be amused at its nature. Try to take your goal seriously without taking yourself seriously.

9

Lovingkindness

gently the sun clears
a tuft of grass for the deer
winter's harsh forage
—MICHO

Three men are driving in the rural Midwest. Late in the day, they're tired and decide to stop at the next motel. To save money, they agree to share a room. The motel owner says that the room will cost thirty dollars. The men each hand the owner ten dollars and proceed to the room. The owner begins to feel bad for charging them thirty dollars when three are sharing a small room. He counts out five dollars and asks his son to return it to the three men. The son, a bit of a dubious entrepreneur, heads for the room and thinks, *These guys will be happy to get anything back. I'll take two dollars for myself and give them one each.* And that's what he did. So, instead of paying ten dollars each, the men paid nine each. Nine times three is twenty-seven, plus the two the boy took, equals twenty-nine. What happened to the other dollar?

When we look at numbers we must look carefully because they can appear to be other than what they really are. The reality is that thirty dollars was paid and five dollars was returned. The men received three back and the son kept two. Viewed correctly, the numbers add up. When we don't see things as they really are, the numbers don't make sense, just as life's ongoing events often don't seem to make sense. But if we see things as they really are, we won't be confused. Life will present its challenges, but we'll have the insight and wisdom to deal with them.

Each of us has undoubtedly performed many acts of kindness, and each of us has occasionally slipped and acted unkindly, so we all have the experience of knowing which feels better, which feels more like the person we want to be. We have the genuine, empirical experience of knowing what brings us happiness and peace, and what brings us unhappiness and stress. We don't want to lose sight of that truth. When we do, things will seem off, like the phantom dollar that was missing at the motel. The Buddha referred to that "off" feeling as *dukkha,* a type of dissatisfaction, discomfort, and disjointedness. The teachings offer remedies for dukkha, one of which is called *metta*, which is translated as "lovingkindness" or "loving friendliness." Metta is a loving, compassionate, and altruistic view of all beings, free from attachment, judgment, expectation, and self-interest. The development and ongoing practice of lovingkindness is seen as a deterrent to anger and negativity. In turn, it makes us more at peace with ourselves and a joyful presence to those around us. Lovingkindness calms the mind, eases the body, and opens the heart. The teachings on lovingkindness refer to a caring for others that is free from all conditions—a caring that is likened to the love of a mother for her only child.

I have a vague memory of my mother as a loving and caring parent—vague because she died when I was sixteen and my childhood was, before and after her death, for the most part, filled with trauma, fear, and disruption. My fondest childhood memories are of my maternal grandmother. She loved her children (four girls) and her grandchildren (seven boys) with an unconditional, bear-hugging, joyfully uplifting affection that could melt the combined forces of Lucifer and Mara. We grandchildren called her Bubbe, the Yiddish word for grandmother. Today I notice the similarity between "Bubbe" and "Buddha." It is said that a fully awakened being—a Buddha—is loving, compassionate, wise, and joyful. As I look back, I cannot help but wonder if my Bubbe was my first experience of a Buddha. The exuberant hugs from this four-foot-nine, silver-haired fireplug still, decades later, caress my ribs and bring a smile to my heart. As she engulfed me in her arms and smothered me close to her, she seemed unable to contain her joy. She would often exclaim something like, *"Ich liebe deinen kopf,"* which I believe translates as "I love your head." It may have been an idiomatic expression, or maybe she just felt that close to me. In any event, these many years later I can still feel the enormity and joyous energy of her love, and when I think of her, my heart opens wide. Her love for her children and grandchildren was unconditional. When we messed up her small apartment, it was fine; our little fingers, greasy from her amazing potato pancakes, were welcome anywhere. Perhaps within her there was uttered a silent *Oy,* but all we heard was, *"Ich liebe deinen kopf."*

Poetically, we usually say that love emanates from the heart. In truth, love is like a spiritual gift that starts in the mind and finds its way through the heart center to physical expression. Its power cannot be overestimated. Consider the impact my grandmother had on her grandchildren and, I suspect, on many others with whom she came in contact. The blessing of her spacious, loving heart reverberates within people today, long after her death—people she never met. So it is with what we put out into the universe. All of our actions have consequences, and those consequences affect the lives of those around us and those who follow after us. My grandmother's love reaches people today through her grandchildren and great-grandchildren, and perhaps through the butterfly effect. (The butterfly effect is a theory that something as small as the wave of a butterfly's wings could have an effect in the future, causing something as large as a hurricane or a tornado.)

The practice of lovingkindness can uplift us and relieve sorrow and unhappiness. When we understand that love is not just a feeling, we see that the emotional experiences we call love are but a small part of what love is really about. We see that we can even love people we don't particularly like. Lovingkindness develops when we do something for another being that benefits their spiritual or emotional growth. We can be angry with someone and still decide to do something nice for them. The natural function of lovingkindness is to enhance friendliness and to dispel anger, hatred, and ill will. Unlike emotional love, the *love* of lovingkindness isn't blind, it just sees what matters.

A Spanish proverb says, "The door to the human heart can be opened only from the inside." Even the greatest of poets cannot describe the depth of love that the human heart can experience. In spiritual practice we refer to the heart center rather than the heart organ. It can be an indicator of what is going on within us. We're so inundated with "just do it" and "go for it" type messages that the energy of just being with another can appear to be doing nothing at all. Yet connecting heart to heart is anything *but* doing nothing. Being in touch with our heart center and making authentic heart-to-heart contact with another require energy and concentration. How do we start? What can we do in our busy lives to be more in touch with our own heart center? We could start by stopping—stopping to take a moment in stillness. We could enjoy a long gentle in-breath and a long outward sigh. (How about right now?) We could lighten up—even a little bit can help. A heart can become heavy both spiritually and physiologically, especially when its companion is a relentless mind. We could walk on the earth (a part that's not paved over with concrete), smell a flower, sing a song, dance with a friend, and offer a smile to that person in the mirror.

My friend Dodger has taught me that it is possible to love everyone. Of course, Dodger is a golden retriever, and that means it is his nature to be enthusiastically loving toward everyone and everything—eating, peeing, pooping, walking, Margaret, Brian, sniffing, Paulette—everything and everyone is exciting and cause for considerable tail wagging. Now, even Dodger has his favorites, particularly those who can't wait to fuss over him and lavish him with delectable goodies. They are greeted with tail wagging of such fervor as to endanger anyone or anything that might happen to be behind him. In some cases, said wagging is accompanied by sensuous moans emanating from the very depths of his furry being. Even though he has his favorites, everyone is approached with his ubiquitous loving enthusiasm. He has no interest in a person's wealth, education, or station, only whether they are interested in sharing some loving friendliness. Of course, sharing an edible treat with him scores extra points, but I've observed his interactions with people for more than ten years, and he is a teacher of the pure joy of loving friendliness. He loves people unconditionally, and they can't help but feel that love. I've seen many a frown turn upside down in his presence.

Our greatest happiness comes from the experience of love and compassion. The more we genuinely care about others, the greater our own happiness and inner peace. So, loving others is the greatest gift we can give ourselves. It's almost a contradiction—altruism that rewards one's self. For each of us, there are those we find easier to love and those we find more challenging. But the practice of being a loving, compassionate person allows no boundaries—no one can be excluded. Those who push our buttons—who appear rude, arrogant, greedy—those are the very people with whom we can refine our practice. No matter how different the look, behavior, customs, or costumes, there is no significant difference among people—a loving, compassionate person recognizes that our basic natures are the same. We all want to be happy, and we all want to be loved.

When I first discovered the Native American flute, I was immediately drawn to its sound, touch, and aroma. I'm an amateur woodworker and find the look, feel, and smell of wood enticing, so the initial attraction was not surprising. Then, when I played the flute for the first time, I was deeply moved by its haunting, mystical quality. My playing is now at a level that I am occasionally invited to play at weddings, funerals, and other events. I have even jammed with some of the best Native musicians in the country. To keep my ego in check, I received a letter from our upstairs neighbors who had just moved in, stating that my flute playing was so annoying that they couldn't even have a conversation without being disturbed by the sound. This set off a whirlwind of thoughts and feelings within me: *The Native American flute is probably the softest-voiced instrument ever created. They must not have their floors covered with carpet or they could never hear my playing. We now have complainers living above us. Will I ever be able to live in peace again?*

There are probably travelers along the spiritual path who would think, *Ah, thank you, dear neighbors, for this opportunity to practice lovingkindness.* I'm afraid I was not yet that advanced. I felt angry and threatened, concerned that this could lead to . . . who knows what? I didn't feel especially grateful for this opportunity to develop my spirituality, but I met it as best I could. Over the next couple of days, I looked to find that place within me from which I could respond with kindness and offer a solution that might be acceptable to everyone concerned. I understand that such solutions are often not completely satisfactory, but I was mindful of my intention when I wrote a reply to their letter. I offered to play, whenever possible, in the daytime when they were at work, and when I did play in the evening, I would play one of my lower-voiced flutes, which are particularly soft-sounding. Unfortunately, one's kindness and efforts are not always accepted graciously. Whenever I cross paths with these neighbors, I always smile and say "Hello," but they don't acknowledge my greetings and usually turn and ignore me. However, I don't feel I have failed. I was clear as to my intentions, and I am clear that I wish for them to be happy. I believe that everyone is the owner of their karma. Their happiness and unhappiness depend on their actions, not on my wishes for them. This is the ground of equanimity practice, which we will look at in the next chapter.

believe that the opposite of love is fear. Fear is an obstacle to love; fear is an opponent of love, and a formidable opponent at that. The Spanish playwright/novelist Miguel de Cervantes said, "One of the effects of fear is to disturb the senses and cause things to appear to be other than what they are." Wisdom is to see things as they really are. Therefore, it would follow that developing a kind and loving heart would help us live more wisely. A useful rule to remember is: if it looks like wisdom but is unkind, it is not wisdom; if it feels like love but is not wise, it is not love. Significantly, love and fear cannot be active in us at the same time. In other words, if we are thinking, speaking, and acting from a truly loving place within, we are not experiencing fear. Conversely, if our thoughts, words, or deeds are fear-motivated, we will not be acting lovingly. At such moments, we might think that if so-and-so didn't act that way, or if such-and-such hadn't happened, we would be happier, which might be so. But circumstances and conditions are as they are, and it is how we experience them that determines our happiness. Louisa May Alcott apparently understood this when she said, "I'm not afraid of storms, for I'm learning to sail my ship."

What most of us want is to be accepted unconditionally for who we are, with our mistakes and unskillfulness. Likewise, we need to accept others for who they are. We need to realize that the wishes, desires, and needs of others are as important to them as ours are to us. To be a loving, compassionate person is to understand that we are all fellow travelers on this journey, that we all experience the joys and sorrows that comprise this adventure called life.

The practice of metta, or lovingkindness, as taught in the Buddhist tradition, is the offering of loving thoughts first to one's self and then, progressively, reaching out to all beings. This practice of offering thoughts of lovingkindness can dissolve fear, anger, and greed, which are the saboteurs of love. The ultimate metta practice is to become a loving person in even the most challenging and abusive situations. This does not mean becoming a doormat but rather one who acts with compassion in any circumstance. In some of us the seed of love may have gone dormant because it has not received the light, warmth, and nutrients needed for its growth. But love is like the sun: no matter how many cloudy days hide its face, it is always there, ready to shine through in the next moment.

Bear in mind that it is not possible to practice

lovingkindness for others without a foundation of self-love. If we try to act compassionately out of a belief that others are worthier than we are, the true source of our actions may be more about self-hatred than compassion for others. Genuine compassion arises from a tenderness we feel for our own distress and sorrows, which we then see mirrored in the sorrows of others. The Buddha taught that you could search the entire universe for someone more worthy of your love and affection than you are yourself, but that person could never be found and that no one is more worthy of your love and affection than you are yourself. Learning to love yourself opens the door to being able to love all beings. Also, we don't offer loving thoughts from a position of superiority or with condescension. We're all in this together, and we all want to be happy.

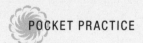 POCKET PRACTICE

Each day, offer thoughts of lovingkindness to yourself and to all beings.

Here is a short version of the lovingkindness practice that I use every day at the end of my morning meditation and before I fall asleep at night. I have added a couple of my own lines not found in the metta discourse.

Think gently to yourself: *May all beings be safe. May all beings be happy. May all beings be healthy. May all beings live with ease. May all beings live in peace. May my life be of benefit to all beings.* (To "live with ease" refers to dealing with our everyday activities—home life, the workplace, the kids, traffic, and so forth—free from stress and turmoil.) If you are going through a difficult period, or if it just feels right, it's fine to focus primarily on yourself: *May I be safe, may I be happy,* etc. If you know of someone who is going through a particularly difficult time, you might want to focus primarily on them; envision them and think, *May you be safe, may you be happy,* etc. It's nice to end by offering metta to all beings: *May all beings be safe,* etc. Feel free to alter the wording so that it feels right for you. Offer the thoughts at a pace that enables you to maintain concentration from one sentence to the next.

POCKET PRACTICE

End each day with thoughts of lovingkindness.

Do the above practice at night. Lying in bed, repeat the phrases until you fall asleep.

 POCKET PRACTICE

When someone is pushing your buttons, replace your annoyance toward that person with the silent wish, *May you be happy*. Notice how it feels.

At times when you become annoyed or impatient—waiting on line at the market, waiting on hold for telephone assistance, getting cut off on the highway, and so forth—offer to the person you feel is the source of your annoyance this gentle, silent thought: *May you be happy*. Repeat as needed, *May you be happy*. Make this a frequent practice, so that it starts to become your regular response to aggression and rudeness. It may feel artificial at first, but that's okay, stay with the practice. With time, lovingkindness can replace anger. Try it with complete strangers you pass on the street. Offer them your thoughts of lovingkindness: *May you be happy*. Notice the feelings that arise with kindness as opposed to those with anger or resentment.

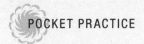

POCKET PRACTICE

> When feeling angry, tense, or anxious, remind yourself that
> these feelings are grounded in fear. Stop and try to identify
> the cause of the fear.

When you experience impatience, resentment, or anger, stop and ask yourself, *All right, what is this fear?* It can be difficult for some of us big guys to acknowledge fear, but it is an absolutely normal feeling and part of the human condition. Ask yourself quietly, "What is this fear?" Remember, thoughts, words, emotions, and deeds not coming from love are likely coming from fear.

POCKET PRACTICE

> When feeling alone and discouraged, recall someone who
> has loved you unconditionally.
>   See their kind face and bask in their presence.

At times we can feel lonely, abandoned, unloved. Bring to mind someone who offered you unconditional love at some time in your life. See that person and hold them in your consciousness for a few moments. If you cannot recall such a person in your life, visualize being in the presence of someone like Jesus or the Buddha, and accept their lovingkindness toward you.

The metta sutta (discourse) is one of my favorites. I find it deeply moving, effective, and quite beautiful. For an in-depth look at the teachings and practice of metta, I highly recommend Sharon Salzberg's classic book *Loving-kindness* (Shambhala, 1995).

Here are just a few lines from the discourse:

> . . . *May all beings be happy. May they be safe and joyful.*
> *All beings, whether young or old, sturdy or frail, male or*
>   *female, wise or misguided,*
> *strong or feeble, visible or obscured, near or far, born or not*
>   *yet born,*
> *may they all be happy . . .*
> *Even as a mother would offer up her life for her child, her*
>   *only child,*
> *thus should one hold dear all living beings, without*
>   *exception, with an unbounded heart:*
> *A source of kindness spreading throughout the entire universe,*

reaching up beyond the stars,
and down below the ocean's depth;
outwards beyond all directions,
unencumbered by any type of aversion, hostility, or loathing . . .
May all beings be happy . . .

In the summer of 2009, I was on safari in Zambia and Botswana. I had been to Africa several times before and had seen many fascinating things, but never had I actually witnessed an animal "kill." (That is the term used for a successful predator hunt.) This time I saw three, up close, from chase to feeding. The sight, sound, and smell of each have remained vividly within memory's reach. To witness these violent acts that are part of the natural order is, in a certain way, a privilege, albeit a difficult one. We know that without killing, wild animals in their natural habitat cannot survive. As one who wishes for all beings to be happy and safe, the sight of such suffering—and there is no doubt in my mind that an animal-turned-meal suffers—was disconcerting.

For weeks afterward I thought about the fact that in my daily metta practice, I wish for something that cannot be. All beings cannot be safe and free from suffering. I questioned this aspect of my practice—whether I was wasting my time and, more important, not dealing with reality. After much reflection, I have, for now, come to

the following conclusions. If one or more of these resonates with you, try the following.

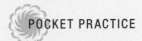

POCKET PRACTICE

Contemplate and accept that there are times when you can
help and times when you cannot. Remember that just feeling
bad helps no one.

Sit quietly for a few minutes each day and reflect on the
following:

- There is suffering in the world, including my own,
  that I can help to relieve, and I will endeavor to
  do so.
- There is suffering in the world about which I can
  do nothing. When I accept that reality, I am more
  available to experience and share my own happiness and that of others. My sadness helps no one.
- I am determined not to add to the suffering in
  the world.
- I, and those around me, fare better when my
  heart and mind are filled with lovingkindness.

10

Equanimity

soon to close its eyes
even the sun gets tired
dreaming of the moon
—MICHO

A modern definition of equanimity: cool. This refers
to one whose mind remains stable and calm in all
situations (as opposed to a spiffy dresser). From
the Buddhist perspective, equanimity is about one's ability to maintain composure, balance, and an impartial
mental state amid life's continuously changing conditions,
a composure that is not shaken by the vicissitudes of
life, such as pleasure and pain, gain and loss, praise and
blame, fame and obscurity.

Sometimes our ability to maintain equanimity can
be seriously challenged. Such was the case when, several

years ago, a woman in Kansas City walked into her favorite Häagen-Dazs store and ordered an ice cream cone. She turned around for a moment and found herself looking right into the face of the actor Paul Newman, who was in town filming *Mr. & Mrs. Bridge.* Stunned by his dazzling blue eyes, her knees wobbled but she managed to turn around, get her ice cream cone and her change, and leave the store. After a few moments she regained her composure and realized that she didn't have her ice cream cone. She went back into the store and again found herself face-to-face with Mr. Newman, who asked, "Are you looking for your ice cream cone?" She nodded yes, and he said, "You put it in your purse with your change."

Under certain conditions, even experienced practitioners can be shaken from their otherwise equanimous state. I had enjoyed a couple of books by the meditation teacher Larry Rosenberg, so when I saw that he would be leading a retreat at Insight Meditation Society, I mentioned it to Susanna, and we decided to attend. These ten-day retreats are held in silence except for the talks offered each evening by the teacher and the one or two short interviews each retreatant has with the teacher. After we were back home for several days, Susanna said to me, "If you promise not to think I'm ridiculous, I'll tell you about something that happened on retreat." Susanna has a Mensa-like intellect and a reputation for being a walking encyclopedia, so it would be difficult to imagine her saying or doing anything truly ridiculous. However, during retreats strange things can happen to the mind. It seems that on about the fifth day, Susanna went to Larry for an interview and told him she was very upset. Larry asked what was troubling her. "I think Allan doesn't love me anymore," said a tearful Susanna. Larry asked why she thought that. "Because he hasn't been speaking to me," answered Susanna. Larry thought about that for a moment and replied, "Well, you know, this is a silent retreat."

As a spiritual practice, equanimity allows us a balanced, spacious insight into the constantly changing nature of all things. Anyone who has raised a teenager knows how quickly "I love you" can turn to "I hate you" and then back again, motivated by nothing more than what another parent is allowing that day that you are not. Equanimity is not shaken by change, no matter how abrupt or traumatic. Though serene, it is active; it is not indifference, apathy, or a dull state of mind. It imbues the other practices we have been exploring with a sense of stability, yet equanimity itself is not any more solid or permanent than any other condition. It is constantly adjusting to the ebb and flow of life and, important, when faltering, it can be regenerated in any given moment. Effort and determination are required to develop equanimity, and then it can be strengthened over and over again through well-practiced mindfulness. It is the gentle, ongoing presence of mindfulness that supports an equanimous mind.

A prerequisite for the development of equanimity is the quality of acceptance, free from attachment and judgment. We all have preferences regarding this and that, but equanimity allows us to accept what comes our way without struggle, distress, or conflict. In other words, when equanimity is present, suffering is not. (Remember that pain and suffering are not the same. It is said that in life, pain is inevitable, but suffering is optional.) I have a friend who often suffers because of the weather. "It's disgusting out," she will say. Then I wonder to myself, *How can the weather be disgusting?* Weather is weather—rain, snow, sun, cold, hot, it's all weather. The weather has no intrinsic good or bad qualities. We may not like rainy days, but that's just preference. Besides, why fuss about something we cannot change? Some weather forecasters, perhaps out of their need to draw an audience, do what some politicians do. They use the fear factor. I remember on January 3, 2008, one announcer said, with great relish in his voice, "Stay tuned for the details of the Blizzard of '08." We had about a half inch of snow, but it was the most snow that had fallen in the new year. Therefore, "the Blizzard of '08."

Suffering is usually related in some way to a desire for things to be different from the way they are, so accepting things as they are is a major step toward happiness. If a situation is not acceptable, the equanimous mind thinks clearly and seeks appropriate possibilities. The mind may perceive a condition as unpleasant, but with equanimity, a spaciousness is opened and solution replaces struggle. When we confuse our view of things with reality, we can lose that spaciousness. "I didn't enjoy that movie" is different from "That was a terrible movie." The former expresses a view and is spacious. The latter is rigid and harsh.

Equanimity is the stable mind that allows us to be present to all conditions, difficult or pleasant, challenging or joyful, while maintaining a calm, radiant peacefulness, a trust that receives the world and all its conditions, knowing that all is as it has to be. "Knowing that all is as it has to be" does not mean that all is as we would like it to be, or that all is pleasant or fair. It means that all circumstances are born of the causes and conditions that precede and accompany them. To change what is unpleasant, unjust, unkind, or unfair, we must change the causes and conditions. The equanimous mind comprehends this and guides us through appropriate action, balanced with kindness and wisdom. It allows us to feel compassion in the face of great suffering without being devastated. We see that there is no condition or circumstance that can be made better by our unhappiness. This view helps us be *in* the world without being *of* the world.

Seeing and accepting that all things are as they are because of the causes and conditions that precede them provides insight into the law of karma. Karma is so profound and of such depth that the Buddha said that no one, except for fully enlightened beings, could possibly grasp its full meaning. However, it is not necessary to completely grasp the meaning of karma, or even to believe in it. Consider the law of gravity. Few among us truly know how it works. We just know that when we drop something it falls down, not up or sideways. All physical things, including us, remain somewhat anchored to the earth because of the force of gravity. You don't have to understand it, and you don't have to believe in it; gravity simply is. It is the same with karma. According to this natural law, all events, conditions, and situations are the result of the actions (karma) that precede them.

Once we understand that in every moment we exist in an extremely complex web of unfolding conditions, we can also see that right now, through wise intention and skillful action, we can create new, more positive conditions. Our past actions have brought us to this moment. Our actions *in* this moment create our future karma, both immediate and long-term. We can create new karma that leads to greater happiness and the end of *dukkha* (suffering, or sorrow).

According to Buddhist teachings, karma is neither predestination nor fatalism, and it is not bestowed upon us by an all-knowing supernatural power. It is the sowing of our own actions bearing fruit upon ourselves. Acts of lovingkindness and compassion will ultimately return lovingkindness and compassion, as unkind words and deeds will ultimately return sorrow and stress. Therefore, we have the potential to make substantial changes in our karma. The extent of such changes is in our own hands, and as with all actions, change begins with our thoughts.

The Buddha taught that intention is karma. Intention leads, and karma is created through, our thoughts, words, and actions. He said, "All beings are the owners of their karma, heirs to their karma, born of their karma, related to their karma, upheld by their karma."

The teachings say further that it is karma that illumi-
nates the entire world, because through it we see the
cause of all happiness and unhappiness, and the path
to the alleviation of our sorrow. When we see things as
they really are, we realize that we no longer have to feel
caught up and tossed about by life's capricious nature.
We are responsible for our own happiness and unhappiness, yet rarely do we see how we cause ourselves so
much grief. Don't be deceived by appearances; things
are not necessarily what they seem to be, and even if
they were, they are constantly changing. Everything is
impermanent. All experience is relative and reliant on
the mind and its perceptions and interpretations. The
responsibility for what we experience lies entirely within
ourselves. Our happiness is dependent on accepting this
and nurturing a kind, loving, and spacious heart. The
essence of the dharma—the teachings of the Buddha—is
about identifying the cause of our suffering and alleviat-
ing it. That cause always comes back to delusion, because
we don't see things as they really are. (That phrase keeps
coming up, doesn't it? Maybe there's something to it.) It is
our perception, our view of the conditions and circumstances in and around us, that determines not only our
happiness but our entire experience of life.

We don't have to feel as though we're drowning with every shift of the tides, which is important to know, because the tides are constantly shifting. Today, in the twenty-first century, science is confirming the Buddha's teaching: nothing is fixed, nothing is solid. Even that which appears solid is apparently just vibrating energy. The physical world as we know it, we are now told, consists only of data contained in energy vibrating at various frequencies. We can't see the world as vibrating energy because it is vibrating much too fast for our senses to register. We take in only bits of energy information and know these bits as "car," "house," "Susan," "tree," "book," and all other visible objects in our perceived universe. *Neuroplasticity*, the recent discovery that tells us, in part, that the fully developed brain can actually change shape in accordance with conditions, may have enormous implications in addressing physical and emotional health. What might have seemed theoretical two thousand five hundred years ago is now being proven true. Everything is constantly changing. Accepting the reality of change gives rise to equanimity. We see that while we cannot control impermanence, or so many other conditions in our lives, we can take responsibility for our experience of all things.

How do we withstand the jarring changes that are part of our relationships? Wasn't it just yesterday that we were so in love with the very person we're now battling in divorce court? How can we suddenly be fantasizing about strangling the dear friend who loaned us the money, interest-free, to start our business? Everything changes— even the most loving, supportive relationships eventually must come to an end—and somehow we go on.

When Susanna and I were considering founding a not-for-profit organization, we had a friend whom I considered quite close. Let's call him Bart. Bart was gracious and generous to us, and used to say that I was "like gold" to him. With his wife, the four of us socialized often, and I always enjoyed our time together. It turned out that Bart didn't want us to start a new venture but instead wanted us to work with an organization with which he was associated. In numerous conversations, we listened attentively to his ideas and gave them considerable thought; however, we eventually made the decision to start the new organization. We explained our reasons to Bart and hoped he would understand, but our decision must have touched something deep within him. He unleashed an attack on us that included sending a flood of hostile e-mails, initiating rumors and gossip, and doing anything he could to discredit us. The intensity of his actions caused me enough concern, particularly for Susanna's safety, that I sought the advice of a psychiatrist who was experienced in this area. After reading Bart's e-mails, he concluded that discretion would be the better part of valor. He advised us to avoid contact with Bart and not to respond to any communications from him. He would probably soon get bored and move on. After about a year things settled down and we stopped hearing from him.

About four years later, I was at an event with several hundred people and I suddenly saw Bart walking toward me. He opened his arms and embraced me for a long time in silence. Then, with moist eyes, he asked for my forgiveness. He said he had no idea what had happened to him back then but added that during that time he had been off his medication. I told him that I had long since forgiven him, and I apologized for anything on my part that I might have handled unskillfully. Our friendship has not rekindled, but at least the door is open to the possibility, and, more important, we are no longer "enemies." When in conflict, it is often wise to wait until the flames cool before attempting to make amends. Then, clearing the air as best we can may go a long way toward lightening the heart and allowing room for the development of greater equanimity.

Here is an equanimity practice that can offer insight into the nature of relationships. First, a word about the term "enemy," as used in Buddhist teachings: "enemy" refers to someone with whom we are not getting along *at the present time.* It is not the potent word "enemy" that political and military leaders use with much vehemence and hostility to describe those with whom a nation or country has seemingly irreconcilable differences.

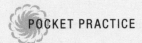

POCKET PRACTICE

Look carefully at what attracts you to some people and why you shun others. Consider whether these feelings come from a limited view and, if so, consider ways to expand your vision.

Sit quietly and visualize before you three people: a friend, an enemy, and a neutral person—someone you might cross paths with regularly but with whom you rarely communicate. Ask yourself why you are attracted to one, feel aversion for the second, and are basically apathetic toward the third. As you contemplate these feelings, can you see that they come from a limited, subjective perspective? Can you see the possibility that each person before you could actually move into one of the other categories, and perhaps already has? We create the relationships we call friend, enemy, and stranger. We generate the conditions in our mind that create "enemy," and we tend to believe what we think.

We can never know the entire story about anyone or anything. Yet how easily we form opinions about others when, in truth, we know so little about them. On an individual basis, we cause ourselves and others so much grief, and globally we have, throughout history, killed untold millions out of sheer ignorance. When people don't look, think, speak, or act as we do, or as we want them to, we can become fearful. We lock our doors, close our minds, chase them from our neighborhood, and attack for reasons we rationalize to be just. How unenlightened we technologically advanced folk can be. No wonder we experience suffering, sorrow, loss, and dis-ease.

For most of us, nothing can disrupt an equanimous mind as quickly as the sudden arising of physical pain. That is not to say that mental and emotional uprisings born of the ever-changing nature of things aren't powerful, but physical pain can capture our attention with an intensity that can be overwhelming. Because we are conditioned to try to push pain away, we tend to have little insight into its complex nature. Pain exists as our experience of particular sensations, usually accompanied by a desire to end the experience. If we observe the nature of painful sensations, we see that they are always changing from moment to moment. What we experience as a continuity of pain is actually a rapidly changing series of sensations. As we practice deeper awareness, we can see how these sensations are changing—sharp to dull, pressure to tingling, aching to throbbing, and so forth. The intensity changes, the temperature changes, the location changes; inherent in the nature of pain is change. We usually miss all of that change because our focus goes to "My pain": "My back is killing me"; "My stomach hurts"; "I have a terrible headache," and so on. This identifying with, and holding on to, something that cannot be owned causes tightening around the pain, thus intensifying the sensations. It is as if we are both grasping and trying to push away the same sensations—a difficult environment for equanimity.

Meditation teachers often offer techniques for focusing on awareness of sensations. Here we will use an adaptation of one of these teachings to create a practice to offset the potential disruption of equanimity caused by physical pain. This practice is not intended to eliminate pain but to alter our experience of it. The sensations may remain, or even intensify, but our relationship to them will change. As an example of how we can relate differently to pain, imagine two people experiencing pain in the stomach. One has just eaten three helpings of rich ice cream with chocolate sauce, nuts, and whipped cream. The other was diagnosed a month earlier with stomach cancer. The former might endure the pain with a simple vow not to overindulge again. The latter might experience extreme anxiety along with the pain. Their physical pain might be very similar, but their relationship to it would likely be quite different.

Because pain can come upon us suddenly and with intensity, regular ongoing practice of this exercise is recommended so that when pain unexpectedly arises, our conditioned reactions can be replaced quickly by more beneficial thoughts and actions. Fortunately, it is not necessary to create physical pain in order to practice. The sensations of a mosquito bite, stiffness in the neck, or an upset stomach are perfect for practice. The exercise also works well with emotional suffering, stress, worry, anxiety, and any other occurrence within the body or mind.

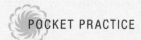

POCKET PRACTICE

Practice calm awareness of physical pain by looking directly at the sensations. Notice how they are constantly changing.

When pain occurs, as quickly and calmly as possible, acknowledge it by identifying it. Say to yourself something like, *Pain is happening (occurring, arising)*. Then take a long, slow breath and begin to observe with detailed awareness the sensations you are experiencing and identify them: *There is stinging, burning, throbbing*, etc. Continue to observe and note the changing sensations (remember, they *are* changing), such as, *The throbbing is intensifying; the stabbing is becoming hot; the tingling is changing to pressure; the sensations are subsiding*. It is likely, but not certain, that the sensations will subside or your mind will move on to something else. (Please note: This is a meditative practice. If the occurring pain is the result of an injury or illness, medical attention may be required. In that case, use this practice as an adjunct to professional care. Wisdom must always prevail.)

The same approach can be taken with stress, unrest, and any form of mental discomfort: *Stress is arising; there is shortness of breath; the palms are moist, there is pounding in the chest*. Continue to observe and note the changing sensations. Try to practice as an interested observer rather than as one to whom the pain or stress is happening. This takes practice, but the skill you develop can be of great value.

After doing the practice, it can be beneficial to write the experience down. As an example: "There was pain. I noted it as 'pain' I noted stabbing, throbbing, burning, and so forth."

The traditional equanimity meditation helps us remember the truth of the impermanent nature of all things, and how all circumstances and conditions come about only though their related causes and conditions. In Buddhism, this is known as "dependent co-arising" (also "dependent origination" or "interdependent arising").

POCKET PRACTICE

Each day, bring to mind that your actions, not your wishes, are the ground of your happiness, both now and in the future.

Find a moment each day to contemplate the following: *All beings are the owners of their karma. Their happiness and unhappiness depend on their actions, not on my wishes for them*. (Of course, the same is true for one's self. My happiness and unhappiness depend on my actions, not on my wishes for myself.)

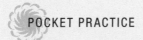

POCKET PRACTICE

> Don't confuse your thoughts, feelings, and perceptions with reality. Practice seeing things as they really are.

Don't believe everything you think. Thoughts are just that—thoughts. They are not reality. Each day, focus on adjusting your thinking so that you will gradually begin to see things more clearly, more objectively. This may require letting go of views and opinions you have held firmly for years. Sometimes an abstract thought to which we are attracted appears in the mind and we invite it to stay. A wise teaching cautions, "The thought manifests as the word, the word manifests as the deed, the deed develops into habit, and habit hardens into character. So watch the thought and its ways with care, and let it spring from love born out of concern for all beings." (Often attributed to the Buddha but it may actually have

been Gandhi who said it.) Don't be swayed by some
thought that happens to drop in for a visit.

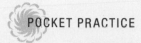

POCKET PRACTICE

Envision your true self. You can love yourself and all beings.

Cultivate these truths: I am kind, I am loving, I am
thoughtful, I am gentle, I am caring, I am compassionate,
I am generous—to all beings, including myself. I can love
everyone, even if I don't like everyone.

POCKET PRACTICE

Close your eyes and contemplate the law of impermanence:
all things are changing; all things die away.

Sit quietly and consider that everything you see before
you is changing and ultimately will pass away. If this
truth is uncomfortable, practice slowly. Let your heart

and mind guide you. The process of dying is not wrong, unnatural, or a failure. Where there is birth there will be death. Acceptance brings equanimity.

Unbelievably, on a sunny Tuesday morning, as I was writing the above lines, my daughter, Samantha, twenty-six weeks pregnant with twins, called from her doctor's office to inform me that one of her babies was no longer alive. A short while later, she; her husband, Sean; Susanna; and I gathered and held one another close for a long time. Stunned and numb, we cried together, and each in our own way struggled to understand and accept. As I held my only child, our broken hearts pressed so close together, my experience of sadness was deeper than I could ever remember. I know that it is the nature of all things to be impermanent; what arises will fade away, and what is born will die. That morning I felt the deep sorrow of seeing that what is not yet born can also die. Spiritual practice does not make us impervious to sorrow, but it can open a bit of space around our deepest wounds, release us from the need to blame ourselves and others, and allow the presence of faith to be felt.

Samantha slumped into a chair, sobbing heavily. Our golden retriever, Dodger, walked over and licked her hand. A gentle smile crossed Samantha's tearstained face.

Epilogue

I t is not easy to live a life on the calm ground of equanimity while the turbulent waters of impermanence are thrashing away with a persistence that at times can seem hell-bent. It takes a great deal of inner work. However, this is what is to be undertaken if we are to experience inner peace and a more joyful life. I believe we are here to be happy, but that doesn't mean happiness will be handed to us. Our happiness and unhappiness depend on our actions, not on our wishes for one another. Yet I do wish you happiness. I wish for you the richness of a generous heart and the dignity of moral behavior. May you know the freedom that comes from letting go and the vision born of wisdom. May your efforts be joyful and your mind be patient. May you be known as one who speaks only the truth, and may great delight emerge from your determination. May your heart be filled with lovingkindness for all beings, and may you enjoy the peace that comes from acceptance and equanimity. Together, may we all complete the spiritual journey.

Acknowledgments

I am deeply grateful to: my editor, Sara Carder, for her expert advice, for making our work on this book a joyful experience, and for simply being the beautiful person she is; Sara's able assistant, Andrew Yackira, for his patience and graciousness; Brianna Yamashita, for her commitment to sharing *Pocket Peace* with the world; Nita Ybarra, for creating a cover that is a glorious work of art; copy editor Amy Brosey and the amazing editorial team, for their amazing skill and eagle eyes; Tarcher/Penguin, for believing in *Pocket Peace* and supporting it with spirit and taste; Loretta Barrett, my elegant and incisive literary agent and an author's best friend; Wayne Muller, for writing the foreword and for offering enthusiastic encouragement from the beginning; Andrew Olendzki, for the immediate and generous sharing of his considerable scholarship; Paulette Callen, for her unstinting approach to the initial line editing; the members of the Community Meditation Center who tried many of these practices and whose comments were invaluable in refining them. The CMC members are a constant source of spiritual stimulation.

I am grateful to Micho, who wrote the Miku poems that open each chapter. Little is known about Micho, but it is believed that he creates his poetry while living quietly near the Delaware River at the foothills of the Catskill Mountains.

I am particularly indebted to the many dharma teachers who have so deeply influenced my life through the years (whether or not they realized it), especially Joseph Goldstein, Andrew Olendzki, Stephen Batchelor, Larry Rosenberg, Yongey Mingyur Rinpoche, Tsoknyi Rinpoche, Thich Nhat Hanh, His Holiness the Dalai Lama, and most especially, Sharon Salzberg, my *kalyana mitta* (spiritual friend), who has been my primary teacher and inspiration since 2002.

Always offering encouragement is my family, Samantha, Sean, and Max, who light up my heart and give me hope for the future.

Finally, my deepest gratitude to Susanna, my perfect partner, who has been with me through the sacred splendor of ten thousand joys and ten thousand sorrows. Through suggesting, encouraging, feeding, humoring, and challenging me, her spirit is woven into the fiber of every page.

The dharma shared in this book is flawless; the author is not. If there is any error, inaccuracy, or unskillfulness in presenting the teachings herein, that is entirely my doing.

Allan Lokos
New York City, 2009

The Pocket Practices

Following is a listing of the Pocket Practices outlined in this book for easy reference.

1. GENEROSITY
   - For one week carry at least five one-dollar bills with you wherever you go, and do not walk past anyone who is asking for help.
   - Greet folks with a smile.
   - Perform spontaneous acts of generosity.
   - Focus intently on what is being said by others, so as to be able to repeat accurately what they have said.
   - From time to time, when you want to ask for more, ask instead, "How can I give more?"

- Work this sentence (or a similar one) into your conversations, especially when there is disagreement: "Let me think about that."

- Contemplate often questions such as, *In what situations am I most likely to stray from my values?*

- Sit with your eyes closed and contemplate one of the five precepts described earlier. Spend time with each one every day for a week and consider its potential benefit in your life.

- For a week, several times a day, as you are about to do something, anything, even the simplest act, ask yourself, *What is my intention?*

- When you touch the phone, about to make a call or send a text message, ask yourself, *What is my intention?* As you are about to enter a meeting, ask yourself, *What is my intention?*

- Envision a person whose moral character you admire and imagine that you are telling them of a decision you are about to make.

- Each day for two weeks, sincerely praise others' words or deeds.

- Take time each day, every day, to practice being the person you want to be.

3. RELINQUISHING

- At least once each year, go through your belongings, choose one that you really like, and designate it to be given away.

- Sit quietly and contemplate these five powerful insights (see page 70). Progress gradually, perhaps working with one contemplation once a month.

- Consider whether it's more important for you to be right or to be happy.

- Consider letting someone off the hook for a deed they committed or harsh words they spoke.

- Once a month for six months, do not eat for half a day.

- Recite the five contemplations (see page 75) before each meal.

4. WISDOM

- On a regular basis, choose a particular situation and practice Beginner's Mind.

- Consider how your discomfort with a particular situation might be eased by accepting things as they are.

- Each evening for two weeks, recall one conversation you had or one action you took during the day. Consider the many possibilities that might result from your words or that action.

- When the words or actions of another elicit anger within you, stop before reacting and ask yourself, *Am I about to speak and act as the person I want to be?*

- Spend time with older folks; they're experienced at doing life.

5. JOYOUS EFFORT

- Once a week, push yourself to do one more repetition or to go five minutes longer on the treadmill than you would ordinarily.

- Spend a few quiet moments at the end of each day considering and encouraging your most positive way of thinking.

- Create a personal one-hour retreat.

- Focus on effort, not results. When facing new and challenging situations, projects, or adventures, take a few moments throughout the day and remind yourself, *I can do this, and I can enjoy it. I will give it my full effort; that's all I can do.*

6. PATIENCE

- Find a place where you can feel completely at ease and say to yourself, *Only I can destroy my peace, and I choose not to do so.*

- Understand and accept that in each given moment, everyone, including you, is doing the best they can.

- Write these words on a dozen little pieces of paper and strategically place them where you'll see them often: "Patience. This too shall pass."

7. TRUTHFULNESS

- Think before speaking, particularly in the presence of children.

- Develop listening skills.

- You need only a one-word practice when it comes to teasing: *don't!*

- Do not speak about anyone who is not physically present.

- Before clicking the send button on the e-mails you write, stop, close your eyes, and breathe for a few seconds.

- When you feel that a conversation is about to become heated, stop and consider what you are about to say before saying it.
- Before going to bed at night, write down one truth you learned that day.
- One day each month, every time you are about to speak, stop for a moment and consider if what you are about to say will improve upon the silence.

8. DETERMINATION

- Remind yourself often that you are mentally strong—you can do it.
- Don't hold grudges—find a way to forgive.
- For five minutes, focus on a specific object, bringing the mind back to the object each time it wanders.

9. LOVINGKINDNESS

- Each day, offer thoughts of lovingkindness to yourself and to all beings.
- End each day with thoughts of lovingkindness.

- When someone is pushing your buttons, replace your annoyance toward that person with the silent wish, *May you be happy*. Notice how it feels.
- When feeling angry, tense, or anxious, remind yourself that these feelings are grounded in fear. Stop and try to identify the cause of the fear.
- When feeling alone and discouraged, recall someone who has loved you unconditionally. See their kind face and bask in their presence.
- Contemplate and accept that there are times when you can help and times when you cannot. Remember that just feeling bad helps no one.

10. EQUANIMITY

- Look carefully at what attracts you to some people and why you shun others. Consider whether these feelings come from a limited view and, if so, consider ways to expand your vision.
- Practice calm awareness of physical pain by looking directly at the sensations. Notice how they are constantly changing.

- Each day, bring to mind that your actions, not your wishes, are the ground of your happiness, both now and in the future.
- Don't confuse your thoughts, feelings, and perceptions with reality. Practice seeing things as they really are.
- Envision your true self. You can love yourself and all beings.
- Close your eyes and contemplate the law of impermanence: all things are changing; all things die away.

Suggested Reading

Batchelor, Stephen. *Buddhism Without Beliefs*

——. *Living with the Devil*

Boorstein, Sylvia. *Pay Attention, for Goodness' Sake*

Brach, Tara. *Radical Acceptance*

Chödrön, Pema. *When Things Fall Apart*

——. *The Places That Scare You*

——. *Taking the Leap*

Epstein, Mark. *Going to Pieces Without Falling Apart*

——. *Thoughts Without a Thinker*

Feldman, Christina. *The Buddhist Path to Simplicity*

Goldstein, Joseph, and Jack Kornfield. *Seeking the Heart of Wisdom*

Gunaratana, Bhate Henepola. *Mindfulness in Plain English*

Kabat-Zinn, Jon. *Wherever You Go, There You Are*

Kalu Rinpoche. *Luminous Mind*

Kornfield, Jack. *A Path with Heart*

Muller, Wayne. *How, Then, Shall We Live?*

——. *Legacy of the Heart*

Nhat Hanh, Thich. *Being Peace*

——. *Peace Is Every Step*

——. *The Miracle of Mindfulness*

Pandita, Sayadaw. U. *In This Very Life*

Rahula, Walpola. *What the Buddha Taught*

Rosenberg, Larry. *Breath by Breath*

Salzberg, Sharon. *Faith*

——. *Lovingkindness*

Sogyal Rinpoche. *The Tibetan Book of Living and Dying*

Surya Das, Lama. *Awakening the Buddha Within*

Suzuki, Shunryu. *Zen Mind, Beginner's Mind*

Letter to the Reader

Dear Reader,

Do you have a Pocket Practice that you find useful and that you might like to share with others? If so, I'd like to know about it. Please feel free to e-mail me at allan@pocketpeace.com.

Peace,
Allan